Christianity and Reason

Christianity and Reason

SEVEN ESSAYS

THEODORE M. GREENE

LEWIS M. HAMMOND

HELMUT KUHN

HOWARD DYKEMA ROELOFS

GEORGE F. THOMAS

WILBUR MARSHALL URBAN

JOHN WILD

Edited by Edward D. Myers

NEW YORK
Oxford University Press
1951

PREFACE

The papers composing this book were, with two exceptions, read at the annual meeting of the Guild of Scholars in the Episcopal Church, held at the General Theological Seminary in New York, 5-7 December 1947.

The Guild was first organized in February 1940; a statement of Basic Objectives was prepared, circulated among the members, revised, approved by the membership, presented to and approved by the House of Bishops at General Convention. The statement may, therefore, be regarded as a sort of highest common denominator of the views of the members.

The Basic Objectives are, briefly, as follows:

The distinctive task of the lay Christian scholar is to help to clarify the central tenets of historic Christianity, as embodied most adequately in the Nicene Creed, and to exhibit the relation of the secular and the religious to one another. It is his task to demonstrate the relevance of Christian doctrine to secular life and pursuits; it is equally his task to demonstrate the contribution of secular achievement to the larger Christian enterprise.

We should attempt to promote among our academic colleagues a far greater realization than exists at present that a knowledge of historic Christianity—as an event, a doctrine, and a tradition of corporate worship—constitutes a vital part of the intellectual and cultural equipment of every genuinely educated person, irrespective of his religious beliefs or disbeliefs.

We should impress on college preachers and chaplains the imperative need today for a definite and affirmative proclamation of the historic Christian faith. Only thus, we believe, can the Christian Gospel be effectively presented to undergraduates, and only thus can their spiritual need, of which they are becoming increasingly aware, be satisfied.

We should recognize the right and duty of Christian teachers in the secular disciplines to discover and make clear, on all appropriate occasions, the relevance of Christianity to their several subjects of instruction. If propaganda be defined as the dogmatic assertion of a single point of view and the deliberate or involuntary suppression or distortion of alternative points of view, we condemn all propaganda, whether religious or secular, as fundamentally incompatible with the academic spirit. And if evangelism be defined as the endeavor to inculcate belief through persuasion, as opposed to honest, competent, and forceful presentation, we believe that evangelism, whether religious or secular, has no place in a lecture room or a classroom. As scholars, we are committed to the impartial, open-minded, and critical search for truth in all its forms; and, as teachers, we conceive it our duty to encourage at all times the student's critical exploration and evaluation of every academic subject. It is for this very reason that the religious and, more specifically, the Christian point of view should be presented to the student on all appropriate occasions, since, otherwise, a predominantly secular emphasis, frequently antireligious and anti-Christian, must result in a serious distortion of the student's total perspective. Our academic goal is enlightenment, and true enlightenment is precluded whenever the approach to a subject with religious or Christian implications is exclusively secular or, as frequently happens, explicitly antireligious.

Though our prime obligation in a secular world is to urge the priority of the Christian faith, it is also our duty to promote, especially in the Christian community, due recognition of man's secular and humanistic achievement. Bearing in mind that it is only within the general framework of Christianity that secular activities can achieve genuine importance, we believe it to be part of our Christian task to foster the secular pursuit of truth in every field and to co-operate in all other constructive humanistic activities. The distinctive character and value of secular truths and humanistic achievements merit analysis and enjoyment for their own sake, and only in proportion as they are understood and fostered can they be made to contribute as richly as possible to Christian doctrine, worship, and conduct. We would emphatically deny the complete autonomy or self-sufficiency of the secular; we do not believe that the human can get along without the superhuman or that man can achieve the good life by his own unaided efforts, at however exalted a cultural plane. But we do acknowledge the importance of secular endeavor, and we conceive it to be our duty, as Christian teachers and scholars, to promote the understanding and support of such endeavors, particularly within the fields of our several major academic interests.

The task envisaged here is perennial, but it is peculiarly urgent today. There is a desperate need for spiritual leadership, especially in the academic world. We are therefore determined to make a resolute effort, both individually and collectively, to preserve and clarify the profile of historic Christianity in our own thinking, writing, and teaching. To do so we must better acquaint ourselves with responsible work in the several fields of Christian scholarship, and we cordially invite scholars in our theological seminaries to assist us in this connection. We are also resolved to do everything in our power to promote constructive secular activities within the general fabric of Christianity; to relate, and to cause to coalesce in fuller experience, the secular and the religious without losing the distinctions between them and with due recognition of the ultimate priority of the Christian faith. These are the Basic Objectives of the Guild.

The Guild has, on the whole, taken the attitude that only those who are at once practicing churchmen, laymen, and scholars of repute in their own fields are eligible for election to membership. Every effort has been made to keep the membership small enough so that, at the meetings, discussion may be intimate and informal.

The general topic for discussion at the 1947 meeting was 'The Nature and Role of Theology,' and each of the four prepared papers was designed to treat one aspect of the general subject.

Each paper was followed by at least two hours of discussion. Based upon the four prepared papers, Mr. Roelofs's deals with some of the issues raised in the discussions; it also makes an independent contribution to the subject. Some will perhaps prefer to read Mr. Roelofs's paper before reading the others, in order to get an over-all view of the subjects treated. Two papers, those of Mr. Kuhn and of Mr. Greene, were not read at the meeting but are included because they so clearly expound other and important aspects of the general theme.

The subject is so general and the variety of views on it so great that each of the papers in this volume can, manifestly, be understood as expressing the view only of its author. None of the essays is understood by the editor or by any of the authors to be representative of the views of all members of the Guild of Scholars or of the Episcopal Church in the United States. No attempt has been made to ensure that the volume represent all the theological positions that are maintained in the Church.

The editor wishes to acknowledge his indebtedness to, and to thank, the following publishers who have very kindly given their permission to print quotations from the indicated works, in which they hold the copyrights:

George Allen and Unwin, Ltd., London, the essay 'The Language of Theology' from Wilbur Marshall Urban's *Humanity and Deity;*

Harcourt, Brace & Co., New York, from T. S. Eliot's *Four Quartets;*

Harvard University Press, Cambridge, from A. O. Lovejoy's *The Great Chain of Being;*

Hodder and Stoughton, Ltd., London, from Karl Barth's *The Knowledge of God and the Service of God* and from Karl Barth's *Credo;*

Longmans, Green and Co., Inc., New York, from L. S. Thornton's *The Incarnate Lord;*

The Macmillan Company, New York, from William Temple's *Nature, Man, and God;*

James Nisbet and Co., London, from W. R. Matthews's *God in Christian Thought and Experience;*

Oxford University Press, New York, from Arnold J. Toynbee's *A Study of History;*

Charles Scribner's Sons, New York, from Karl Barth's *Credo;*

The Westminster Press, Philadelphia, from Emil Brunner's *Revelation and Reason,*

and to any other authors and publishers whose names may have been inadvertently omitted.

EDWARD D. MYERS

Lexington, Virginia
January 1951

Mr. Greene is Master of Silliman College and Professor of Philosophy at Yale University. His baccalaureate degree was taken at Amherst College, 1918; his Ph.D. at the University of Edinburgh, 1924; he was formerly McCosh Professor of Philosophy at Princeton University and Visiting Professor in the Humanities at Leland Stanford University. He has written *The Arts and the Art of Criticism* (1940), *The Meaning of the Humanities* (1938), and *Liberal Education Re-examined* (with others, 1943); and he has contributed to other books, and has published many articles in philosophical, educational, and religious journals. His essay originally appeared in much briefer form in the April 1949 issue of *The Atlantic Monthly.*

Mr. Hammond is Professor of Philosophy at the University of Virginia; his baccalaureate degree was taken at the University of Virginia, 1928; his Ph.D. at Virginia in 1932, after a year at the University of Hamburg; he was a member of the faculty at St. John's College, Annapolis, for two years. He has written *Knowing and Making* (University Virginia Studies, 1941) and has contributed many articles to philosophical and theological journals.

Mr. Kuhn is Professor of Philosophy at Erlangen. His Ph.D. was taken at the University of Breslau, 1923. He was formerly

Dozent at the University of Berlin (1930-37), Professor of Philosophy at the University of North Carolina (1938-47), and Professor of Philosophy at Emory University (1947-49). He has written *Die Kulturfunktion der Kunst* (1931), *Sokrates* (1934), *A History of Aesthetics* (with K. E. Gilbert, 1939), *Freedom Forgotten and Remembered* (1942).

Mr. Myers is Professor of Philosophy at Washington and Lee University; his baccalaureate degree was taken at Roanoke College, 1927; his Ph.D. at Princeton, 1931; he was formerly professor at Trinity College, Hartford, visiting lecturer at the University of Cincinnati, and Dean and Professor in the Humanities at Roanoke College. He has written *The Foundations of English* (1940) and has contributed many articles to various journals.

Mr. Roelofs is Obed J. Wilson Professor of Ethics and Head of the Department of Philosophy in the University of Cincinnati. His baccalaureate degree was taken at Michigan, his Ph.D. at Harvard. He has contributed regularly to *Mind*.

Mr. Thomas is Professor of Religious Thought at Princeton University. He took his bachelor's degree in liberal arts at Southern Methodist University, 1919, and in theology at Oxford University in 1923, where he was a Rhodes Scholar. He received his Ph.D. at Harvard University, 1929. He was formerly Professor of Philosophy at Dartmouth, at Swarthmore, and at the University of North Carolina. He has written *Spirit and Its Freedom* (1938) and edited *The Vitality of the Christian Tradition* (1944).

Mr. Urban is Professor of Philosophy, Emeritus, at Yale University. His baccalaureate degree was taken at Princeton, 1895; his Ph.D. at Leipzig, 1897. He was formerly Reader in philosophy at Princeton, Professor at Ursinus, Trinity, and Dartmouth. He has written *Valuation: Its Nature and Laws* (1909); *The Intelligible World: Metaphysics and Value* (1929); *Fundamentals of Ethics* (1930); *Language and Reality* (1939). The paper here included is material from Professor Urban's forthcoming book,

Humanity and Deity, to be published by Messrs. George Allen and Unwin of London. Permission to include it has been given by the publishers, and the editor is very grateful for their courtesy.

Mr. Wild is Professor of Philosophy at Harvard University. His baccalaureate degree was taken at the University of Chicago, his M.A. at Harvard, and his Ph.D. at Chicago, 1926. He has been a member of the Harvard faculty since 1927. He has written *George Berkeley* (1936), *Plato's Theory of Man* (1946), and *Introduction to Realistic Philosophy* (1948).

CONTENTS

○

Preface   v
    EDWARD D. MYERS
Biographical Notes   xi

Man, in the Twilight, Need Not Falter   3
    THEODORE M. GREENE
The Present Relevance of Catholic Theology   18
    JOHN WILD
Theology and Philosophy   36
    GEORGE F. THOMAS
The Language of Theology   57
    WILBUR MARSHALL URBAN
Theology as Theoretical and Practical Knowledge   79
    LEWIS M. HAMMOND
Theology in Theory and Practice   99
    HOWARD DYKEMA ROELOFS
The Wisdom of the Greeks   145
    HELMUT KUHN

Christianity and Reason

Man, in the Twilight, Need Not Falter

BY THEODORE M. GREENE

○

In an article entitled 'Man Against Darkness' in the September 1948 issue of the *Atlantic,* Professor Walter Stace, of Princeton, eloquently defended the following thesis. Science, he argued, has killed religion. It has not merely rendered out of date some of the details of older theological dogmas, forcing their restatement in new, intellectual frameworks. Its destructive impact on religion has been much more radical than that. By destroying 'the old comfortable picture of a friendly universe governed by spiritual values' it has killed, once for all, 'the essential religious spirit.' 'That spirit cannot survive destruction of belief in a plan and purpose of the world, for that is the very heart of it. Religion can get on with any sort of astronomy, geology, biology, physics. But it cannot get on with a purposeless and meaningless universe.'

Unlike many other naturalists who would accept this major premise as a correct statement of fact, and in company with 'the Bishops,' Professor Stace believes that this 'ruin of the religious vision' has produced the 'ruin of moral principles and indeed of all values.' 'No one any longer effectively believes in moral principles except as the private prejudices either of individual men or of nations or cultures. This is the inevitable consequence of the doctrine of ethical relativity, which in turn is the inevitable consequence of believing in a purposeless world.' Another fruit of the scientific spirit is loss of belief

3

in the freedom of the will and moral responsibility. Curiously enough, Professor Stace himself does not believe that the relativity of morals and the denial of freedom are logical implications of a purposeless universe, but he is convinced that the scientific postulate of mechanistic determinism has and must weaken 'moral controls' and a sense of personal responsibility.

Professor Stace concludes that 'it would therefore look as if the early death of our civilization were inevitable,' for our civilization cannot live without ideals, and the religious basis in which our ideals, or moral ideas, have been rooted has been hopelessly undermined. All of the commonly proposed remedies are useless. Philosophers cannot save us because they cannot agree among themselves and because their influence is, in any case, practically negligible. A return to belief in a Christian God and the rise of a new religion are equally impossible because, for the first time in human history, religion itself (not merely this or that religious dogma) is dead—'the light will not shine again.' And it is utterly naïve to suppose, with Professor Dewey, that 'science, which is basically the cause of our spiritual troubles, is likely also to produce the cure for them.' Our only recourse, therefore, is to face the truth and learn to live with it, not because 'truth in the abstract' has any sanctity or supreme value, but because 'in the end we cannot do anything else but face it.' A few individuals have achieved this honesty and maturity. Can the human race grow up as some individual men have grown up? If so, 'all may yet be well'; if not, man will probably 'take a humble place once more among the lower animals.'

I have restated Professor Stace's argument so fully, and with so many quotations, because his position can be discussed fairly only if the several steps in his argument are examined one by one. Indeed, I must urge the reader to read, or reread, his entire article in order to assure himself that I am not unwittingly misrepresenting him in what follows.

Professor Stace has, it seems to me, done us all a very great service in stating a widely held position with a simplicity and clarity which I shall find it very hard to equal. I also want to record my complete agreement with him on two points. He is certainly right that the issue he raises is the crucial issue of our times, and that the crisis he describes is of major importance to us as individuals and to our whole culture. This is no time for smug complacency or superficial optimism. He is right also in insisting on the imperative need for an honest facing of the truth, and a courageous and mature living with the truth. The question is, is 'the truth' what he thinks it is? Is his analysis of our cultural predicament correct? This is the question we must now consider as honestly and courageously as we can.

Let me start with the suggestion that Professor Stace's thesis is far more controversial than the tone of his article, and many phrases in it, would imply. Had he been defending his case in a technical, philosophical journal, he would doubtless have spoken in a more guarded fashion and with less dogmatic assurance. Yet even in a popular article he might well have exemplified the tentative and open-minded scientific temper which he so rightly eulogizes. Professor Stace is certainly entitled to his own opinion; he is certainly justified in expressing it as cogently and persuasively as possible—indeed, he is obligated to do so; but he is not justified in giving the layman the impression that this is a closed issue or that these conclusions are indubitable facts that no intelligent and well-informed man can today question. His high-handed dismissal of idealistic philosophies as 'simply philosophical expressions of romanticism' which have 'perished . . . though of course they still have a few adherents' is sheer dogmatism, reflecting the new pseudo-scientific orthodoxy and the admittedly dominant climate of opinion in some sophisticated intellectual circles, but wholly at variance with the spirit of scientific inquiry and dispassionate philosophical reflection. I am harsh in my criticism of this attitude because naturalists like him have been increasingly guilty of a dogmatism that is scientifically, philosophically, and democratically insufferable.

Professor Stace, and those who agree with him, may be right, and if they are, their advice in regard to what remains to us to do should be most seriously considered. But he and they may be wrong, profoundly wrong, both in their major premises and on specific points, and there are many honest, intelligent, and well-informed people who believe they are profoundly wrong.

Let us at least remember the fallibility of all human judgment, the limits of all human knowledge, and the precariousness of all acts of faith, religious and irreligious alike, and try to exhibit a humility consonant with the mystery of a universe whose ultimate nature the wisest of men can only dimly adumbrate! I, for one, can merely record an opinion, contrary to Professor Stace's, which is no more certain than his, but which I hope is no less informed or honest.

Coming now more closely to grips with the argument, we must distinguish between Professor Stace's sociological description of a major cultural trend and his philosophical acceptance of basic antireligious tenets. On the one hand, he is venturing a historical generalization and prophecy; on the other, he is accepting and defending the thesis that science logically requires an intelligent man to dismiss religious belief as illusory. Either belief can be accepted, rejected, or modified independently of the other.

How accurate is Professor Stace when he says that the 'new imaginative picture of the world' has destroyed 'not merely the outward forms of the religious spirit, its particularized dogmas, but the very essence of that spirit itself, belief in a meaningful and purposive world'; and, further, that Christianity cannot be revived and that a new religion cannot be born? This naturalistic picture of the world is certainly not 'new'—in our tradition it is at least as old as Democritus and Lucretius. Yet, in the minds of many people, it has received the endorsement of modern science, and, with its prestige thus greatly enhanced, it has profoundly influenced the thought and unconscious attitudes of a lot of people, particularly the intelligentsia, but also, in a vague sort of way, the man on the street. This can be confirmed, for example, by any high-school teacher or college professor in close touch with his students.

But this is not the whole story. Not only has organized religion lost no ground during the last decades; it is actually evoking greater interest and receiving more support in this country, in England, and in some portions of Europe than it did during the early 'thirties. More people are going to church with, in many cases, a deeper sense of spiritual need. Theological seminaries are crowded with students who are, on the whole, abler than their pre-war predecessors, and even so, the seminaries are unable to satisfy the demand of churches for more clergy. Missionary activity is increasing in scope and improving in quality, and the ecumenical movement is making rapid strides. There is also increasingly evident in the Church a tendency to take stock of the inadequacies and failures of organized religion, to indulge in contrite self-examination, and to seek to promote a revitalization of belief, thought, and social action. This does not mean that the Church is all it should or might be. It is still bedeviled by conventionality, ritualism, self-righteousness, uncharitable intolerance, and pride. Nor can I see any signs of any major religious revival. I merely dispute the factual accuracy of Professor Stace's generalization that organized religion is at present on the decline. This generalization simply ignores the very large number of clergymen and laymen whose religious life is becoming increasingly sincere and intelligent.

No less significant is the renewed interest of college students in religion. After the First World War the vast majority of them were apathetic or openly hostile to religion. Today an ever-increasing minority is turning to religion in the hope of finding a faith they can live by. Most of these eager inquirers are abysmally ignorant of the Bible, Christian doctrine, and the Christian tradition. Many of them are highly critical of Christian orthodoxy and traditionalism and are righteously indignant at what they regard (often justly) as self-righteousness, wishful thinking, and cant in organized religion. Few are properly equipped to grapple intelligently with the basic problems of religious faith in our secular society. But they are neither complacent or dogmatic; they are deeply troubled and sincerely anxious to find whatever light and strength religion can provide. In short, these young men and women are not systematically debarred from serious religious inquiry by 'the new imaginative picture of the world.' The 'spirit of religion' is not dead in them; on the contrary, it is a vital force in their lives.

Meanwhile, however accurate or inaccurate may be Professor Stace's account of the present trend and temper, I fail to see how he can anticipate the future with such assurance. He seems to be quite certain that 'the light will not shine again. . . Even if a new prophet and a new religion did appear, we may predict that they would fail in the modern world.' He may be right. I, for one, lay claim to no prophetic powers. Our civilization may indeed be headed for an early death; Toynbee seriously envisages that possibility. But Toynbee does not believe that it is 'inevitable,' and I am at a loss to see how Professor Stace, as a proponent of cautious and tentative scientific prediction, can be so certain regarding the historical future. Should he not say rather that much depends upon what we, individually and corporately, believe and do, now and during the next critical years?

This brings me to Professor Stace's crucial contention that science is the only road to truth, that science can know nothing of God or objective values, and that belief in God is therefore no longer intellectually honest. He also insists that 'competent' philosophers can show that the argument against free will and responsibility is a 'tissue of fallacies' and that 'neither the relativity of morals nor the denial of free will really follows from the grounds that have been supposed to support them.' I welcome this latter assertion, and I am sorry that Professor Stace was unable, for lack of space, to explain what kind of free will he deems credible and what 'genuine secular basis for morals' he thinks possible. His own acceptance of the view that the universe is purposeless, meaningless, and indifferent to human welfare, as well as his scornful repudiation of philosophical 'idealism,' would seem to preclude a belief on his part that moral values are in any real sense objective, and to compel his own endorsement of the complete relativity of morals. His insistence that this is not the case, and his further admission that 'science can never tell us what ends to pursue,' may justify the hope that he may be sympathetic to the following interpretation of both moral and religious beliefs.

My own position can obviously not be defended, or even stated, at all adequately in a brief popular article. All I can do is to indicate an approach to the problem very different from Professor Stace's approach, and leading, if it is valid, to a very different final estimate of religious belief. For simplicity, I shall try to state my case in several successive steps.

1. The scientific method has amply demonstrated its validity and power in the areas of inquiry and for the purposes for which it has been designed. Witness the spectacular advance of science over the past three hundred years, the large measure of agreement among reputable scientists, and the technological achievements of applied science, every one of which is a pragmatic demonstration of the scientist's understanding of the natural processes involved. The position I would defend is in no sense an antiscientific position.

2. Science does invite, and support, embracing philosophical accounts of the nature of the physical world in which we live and of which we are a part, and no responsible interpretation of reality as a whole can ignore, or even contradict, careful philosophical generalizations based upon well-established scientific conclusions. Not only, therefore, is the position I would defend not antiscientific; it is committed to reliance upon scientific evidence and to the full incorporation of accepted scientifically supported interpretations of nature.

3. Science, however, in the stricter sense of the term, is not all-inclusive; it addresses itself to a specific type of inquiry into a specific area of reality for a specific purpose. Pure science concerns itself solely with temporal events, both 'physical' and 'psychophysical'; it studies these in order to discover and formulate recurrences and uniformities, commonly called 'laws of nature'; and it does so partly to satisfy man's native curiosity, partly to facilitate his 'control' of nature for greater human welfare. But, as Professor Stace admits, science is by its very nature unqualified to deal with values; it 'cannot give us any ideals'; 'it can teach us the best means for achieving our ends, it can never tell us what ends to pursue.' This fact is enormously important, for it means that science, in its strict sense, can neither prove nor disprove God or goodness or beauty. It simply has nothing to say on these subjects.

Hence the 'imaginative picture of the world' that science, in and of itself, supports is of course a picture of a valueless, meaningless universe. How could it be otherwise? But this does not prove that there are no values and no God in the universe; it proves merely that science cannot possibly discover these values and this Deity if they do exist. If you go fishing with a net designed to catch large fish, the fact that you find no minnows in the net does not prove that there are no minnows in the sea, nor of course does it prove that there are. You have to use a different kind of net to prove that minnows do, or do not, actually exist.

Furthermore, no scientific conclusions, at any point in history, are final, definitive, or certain. They are necessarily hypothetical and tentative. It follows that philosophical extrapolations of science are equally tentative and hypothetical. For example, late nineteenth-century science supported the philosophical doctrine of strict mechanistic determinism; some qualified philosophers today are not sure that the latest scientific thinking justifies any such philosophical conclusion. (This may be what Professor Stace has in mind when he says that 'free will' can still be defended.) In any case, the farther science advances, the less disposed are first-rate scientists to believe that they have fathomed the mysteries even of the world of nature, let alone the whole of reality. Their attitude is humble and cautious, not dogmatic and assured.

4. Professor Stace would, I believe, agree to all this and still repudiate religious belief on the ground that there is no way, comparable to the way of science, of finding God. This, then, is the crucial question for which I believe there is an affirmative answer. Though the religious 'way' to God was known and followed centuries before the development of modern science, we can profitably, in our secular age, indicate its nature by taking our clues from science.

The scientific method is, in essence, the method of rational interpretation of sensory evidence. (I shall ignore here the complications raised by psychology.) This means that both sensory evidence and rational interpretation are essential for scientific knowledge; that sensory data without interpretation are blind, and that reasoning, however consistent, which is not based on sensory evidence is empty of content. Actually, our everyday knowledge of physical objects is similarly an interpretation of what our senses reveal to us. What science has done is enormously to extend and refine both sensory observation (particularly with the aid of controlled experiments) and the interpretation of such observation (so far as possible with the aid of mathematics). The scientific test of truth is therefore always this: is the theory in question logically consistent, internally and in relation to other accepted theories, and does it do full justice to all the relevant, available, sensory evidence? Similarly, on the assumption that scientific observations somehow put us into firsthand contact with nature, and that nature is orderly, most scientists believe that science progressively reveals to us the structure of a reality that we actually confront in our sensory contacts with it. (I say 'most scientists' because there are some scientists and philosophers who deny that even science can tell us anything about an independently real world, and that its only function is to enable prediction and technological control.)

5. If, then, we can accept the basic scientific assumption that the logical interpretation of sensory evidence gives us an ever-increasing understanding of the world of nature, can we not extend this assumption to read that the logical interpretation of moral and religious data, if such exist, can give us an ever-increasing understanding of a 'spiritual,' that is, a moral and religious, dimension of reality which is related to, but not identical with, the world of nature? If this were possible, it would then be the task of philosophy to try to give an account of reality which does justice both to sensory and to moral and religious experiences, to science and to ethics and theology at their best.

The crucial point in the entire constructive argument is thus the concept of 'experience.' If the only type of experience which can be taken seriously—that is, accepted as providing contact with reality and clues to its nature—is sensory experience, then Professor Stace's conclusions inevitably follow. But why must experience be so narrowly defined? What is to prevent us from being really empirical and believing that man's moral and religious experiences, which are no less coercive, vivid, sharable, and rationally interpretable than are his sensory experiences, provide further contacts with reality and further clues to its nature?

Reflective religious faith (in contrast to blind superstition and uncritical faith) rests upon precisely this more liberal and inclusive conception of experience. It is always anchored in primary religious experiences of the individual believer, set in the context of the primary religious experiences of other individuals in the same and in other religious traditions. That is, it is never a mere idea or ideal free-floating and detached from firsthand religious experience; rather, it rests on the deep conviction of all reflective religious believers that only in and through such experiences do we confront a living God. But faith, if it is reflective, is never identified with mere experience, however intense, however often repeated, and however widely shared by others. The factor of reasonable interpretation is as essential as is the factor of the primary experience itself. Without such critical theological interpretations, religious experiences are as 'blind' and as unreliable as a basis for a faith in God as are mere sensations 'blind' and unreliable as a basis for a faith in nature.

6. What we actually find in the history of religions, therefore, parallels what we find in the history of science. The earliest attempts in our tradition at a 'scientific' understanding of nature were those of the pre-Socratic thinkers who tried to explain the whole of nature in terms of one or more of the four 'basic elements'—earth, air, fire, and water. Only very gradually did this attempt grow out of its primitive crudities into the rich pattern of concepts, principles, and methods that constitute modern science. Similarly, primitive religious beliefs and practices were crude, uncritical, and superstitious; it is only gradually that religious experience and belief have developed into what we find them to be, at their best, in the higher religions.

I do not wish to press this analogy between science and religion too hard. Pure science is merely a way of knowing; religion is a way of life based on a way of knowing. Science can use quantitative measurement as theology cannot. And scientists, at least in principle, can hope for a degree of mutual understanding and agreement which theologians in the several major religious traditions, and indeed within any given tradition, have not achieved and are not likely to achieve in the foreseeable future. This disagreement, however, need not invalidate the belief that man can in some measure know God. It is due in part to the inexhaustibility of the Divine nature and man's inability to apprehend it with his finite mind, in part to the great difficulty men of religion have always had in rising above dogmatic utterance and in achieving an attitude of humble, open-minded search. I must admit the unusual temptation in religion, just because it involves man's relation to God Himself, to dogmatism and intolerance for conflicting beliefs regarding the Deity. I do insist, however, on the validity of the religious quest—the belief that man can and does encounter the Divine, that he can and should reflect upon these encounters, and that such reflection can progressively increase his understanding of God and render his belief in Him less superstitious and more responsible and mature.

Many people feel obliged to repudiate religious belief because they identify religion with one of its cruder, more superstitious forms, or because they interpret more enlightened religious beliefs and practices in a crudely anthropomorphic manner. I do not wish to judge Professor Stace's conception of Christianity on the basis of a single phrase, but I was struck, in reading his article, by his repeated reference to 'God in the sky.' If he thinks that an enlightened Christian believes that God is literally in the sky, or that the phrase in the Nicene Creed, 'sitteth on the right hand of the Father,' literally means that God has a body with a right and a left hand, he must of course, as an intelligent man, reject such rubbish. It is true that most professing Christians are deplorably uninformed regarding the language of religious utterance and inclined to a crude anthropomorphism in their thinking about God. But the fact that most people are also scientifically illiterate does not justify us in reading this illiteracy into science and in repudiating science on that score. Similarly, Christianity at its enlightened best should not be identified with its unenlightened distortions. To do so is to throw out the baby with the bathwater—to reject what is quite valid by confusing it with its unjustifiable misinterpretations.

Let us therefore be fair to religion before we decide to brand all religious faith as the 'Great Illusion.' We can and should distinguish man's everyday encounters with nature and his unscientific conceptions of physical objects from the scientist's much more precise observations and much more critical interpreta-

tions of them. We need not, in making this distinction, condemn
the common man's experiences or beliefs as illusory, but we
should recognize their limitations. We can say that he possesses
'opinions' rather than 'knowledge,' defining opinions as beliefs
which may be valid so far as they go but which a man who is
unable to rise above opinions cannot rationally refine or test.
Similarly, we can and should distinguish between the common
man's coercive religious experiences, which he rather crudely
interprets in terms of an inadequate theology, and the far deeper
experiences of the saint and the far more refined interpretations
of the competent theologian and philosopher of religion. This
does not mean that the religious beliefs of the common man are
false, or that he fails to find strength and joy in his religious life;
it does not mean that Christianity is available only to intellectual and spiritual aristocrats. Far from it—witness Jesus' concern for children and uneducated people: 'Come unto me all ye
who travail and are heavy laden.' But Jesus was also concerned
to eradicate inadequate conceptions of God in the minds of his
disciples; and those of his followers who were able to do so
have, for twenty centuries, labored to refine and clarify man's
understanding of God—witness the long history of progressive
theological clarification. Every honest man must of course make
his own final decision as to what he believes and what his ultimate loyalties are to be; but a man is less than honest with himself if he fails to undertake to inform himself what Christianity,
or any other religion, is at its *best* before he rejects it as illusory.

7. I must add one word regarding the vexed problem of authority. The position I have been sketching, most inadequately,
might be labeled 'liberal Christian Protestantism.' This position
is, on the question of authority, at variance with Christian positions which assert the literal truth of every word of the Bible or
the infallibility of certain ecclesiastical dogmas. These claims
to absolute certainty do not seem to me to be credible. I cannot
recognize the 'absolute' authority of either a book or a church.
In company with all such authoritarians I do, however, recognize the impressive authority, in a nonabsolutistic sense, of the
accumulated wisdom of the Church, and of the Bible as a
uniquely rich and revealing record of authentic religious experi-

ences and vital beliefs; and I also agree with those who believe that Jesus taught 'as one having authority.' Such a belief is not only completely credible; it is, to me, quite inescapable. This authority of the Bible (interpreted in the light of the best available Biblical scholarship) and of the Church (interpreted in the light of the best, religiously informed, historical wisdom) and of Jesus Christ, encountered not only in the New Testament but in Christian devotion through the centuries and today by countless sincere Christians—this authority is an enormously impressive testimony that the venture of Christian faith is not illusory, escapist, or irrational; that, on the contrary, it is magnificently rooted in the poignant experience of Christian love, and helpfully elucidated in enlightened Christian doctrine. This faith is not, I believe, to be confused with omniscience or infallibility —it is still faith, not absolute knowledge. But it need not be blind faith, superstitious and irrational; it can become for each individual and for mankind more and more deeply rooted in experience, more and more enlightened, more and more productive of that reflective commitment which is the essential mark of responsible maturity.

I conclude with a list of 'remedies' quite different from those Professor Stace lists and then labels 'useless,' and with a final note of hope rather than despair. I grant that by their disagreements philosophers do weaken their total impact upon society, and that their immediate influence is practically negligible. But I cannot agree that their long-range influence is slight. Philosophical thinking does seep down into a society and both articulates and helps to mold opinion. During the last centuries philosophers have actually contributed greatly to the present pattern of beliefs, which Professor Stace describes, corroborates, and deplores. I heartily second Professor Stace's wish that secular-minded philosophers would 'try to discover a genuine secular basis for morals,' but I also wish that more philosophers today would explore the claims of religion more open-mindedly, empirically, and critically. If they did so, they would help to dispel current confusions and to clarify basic issues.

The churches, meanwhile, could do much more than they are

doing now to educate their clergy and laity, to vitalize the Christian experience of their people, to translate Christian belief into social action, to combat racial prejudice and social privilege within the Christian community, and, above all, to cultivate the tolerance and the humility that should be the first fruits of Christian love. Were the Christian leaven in the churches purer and more powerful, it would be more effective in quickening the religious spirit, which today, though far from dead, is certainly too often dormant and lethargic.

Scientists, in turn, could use their great prestige in our society to clarify the proper nature, objectives, and self-imposed limitations of their scientific method; to emphasize the inability of science, in principle, to validate or invalidate values and human ends; and therefore to make explicit the error of basing our entire philosophy upon science alone. Many leading scientists are today doing just this, and they are rendering our society a great service. On the whole, it is not the scientists who preach a dogmatic naturalism but the lay and professional philosophers.

My final word to Mr. Stace, then, is this: Man finds himself today not in 'darkness' but in a cultural and spiritual twilight which T. S. Eliot describes as a 'place of disaffection . . . in a dim light,' a state of 'neither plentitude nor vacancy,' 'a twittering world.' It may be that we must, as Eliot believes we must, 'descend lower' into

> Internal darkness, deprivation
> And destitution of all property,
> Desiccation of the world of sense,
> Evacuation of the world of fancy,
> Inoperancy of the world of spirit

before we can hope, as individuals or as a race, to achieve the requisite sense of need and the humility necessary, in the words of W. H. Auden, 'to see our salvation.' The Christian Gospel directs us not to a romantic primrose path of comforting illusions, but to the painful road of suffering and sacrifice, to the way of the Cross. Men have never really *lived* by illusions—they have existed, in some kind or other of fool's paradise. Men cannot now really live, fully and deeply, on illusions: either the 'minor' illusions of 'fame, glory, power, or money,' which Professor Stace rather cynically invites us not to give up, or the Great Illusion, which he identifies with religious faith but which should perhaps be identified rather with stygian disbelief in God. We are indeed 'standing on the brink.' We do indeed need courage and honesty, not to face an inevitable loss of faith but to search our own hearts and minds to see whether we ourselves may not have generated this 'darkness' and inadvertently invented the myth that the 'light can never shine again.' We ourselves must assume the responsibility of deciding whether to believe the grim injunction: 'Since faith is impossible and civilization doomed, resign yourself to quiet contentment and be thankful for small mercies—this is the test of secular maturity'; or, alternatively, the sober injunction to achieve a realistic Christian maturity and joy: 'These things I have spoken unto you, that in me ye might have peace. In the world ye shall have tribulation: but be of good cheer; I have overcome the world.'

The Present Relevance of Catholic Theology

BY JOHN WILD

○

As I understand it, the task assigned to me is that of attempting to express and to defend a Catholic interpretation of Anglicanism against certain other alternatives now represented in the Anglican Communion. In spite of my sense of profound inadequacy for the proper performance of this rather overwhelming task, I welcome the general topic of discussion, and hope that with variations it can be continued in the future. What, indeed, is more essential to us as a Guild of Scholars in the Church than frankly to express the points of view which now divide us, and to discuss them together without that false mitigation which spoils all argument, in the hope at least of deepening our own understanding, and at best of arriving at some possible approximation to agreement?

Our civilization is deeply sunk in its 'time of troubles,' to use that vivid expression of Toynbee in his suggestive and, I may venture to say, his very Anglican study of history. How Anglican?—in its readiness to accept all the results of disciplined scientific investigation, to dwell upon them, and yet at the same time to see in them a basically religious pattern; in its negative verdict on the use of force and regimentation of any kind; in its rejection of metaphysical and theological determinism, its insistence upon the reality of challenge and choice in human history, and yet at the same time in its deep discernment of an overarching pattern. Without mentioning the well-known chapter on Gregory VII and investiture, we might also add Toynbee's well-buttressed historical judgment that Western culture, as against Hellenic culture, is based upon Christian principles, and his ability to state sublime and majestic truths in a language intelligible to the people. I regard the publication of this work, therefore, as an event of major importance to the Guild, well worthy of the close attention it has received from several of our members. It deserves our most careful study, and I think will prove to have many apologetic uses.

But it is of course in the last pages of this abridgment of six volumes (which one of our members in a triumphant abridgment of abridgment has now summarized in a two-page chart) that Toynbee's basic religious categories become most clear. Here, in describing the active mode of response to its time of troubles, the only one, if we may trust the light of history, to which a civilization long reeling in disintegration may look with any measure of hope, he uses five categories with an unmistakable Catholic ring—the sense of sin, asceticism, the sense of unity of all mankind under God, martyrdom, and finally that culminating transfiguration by which men can yield up their swollen libidos to something greater than themselves, which is able to infuse them, and through them even a tottering culture, with the fire of present life.

But instead of this, most of us take a more passive course, which has been often repeated by those living in a disintegrating civilization. Instead of the sense of sin which goads us to responsibility and effort, we drift with the current, abandoning ourselves to impulse, and consoling ourselves by great myths of scientific determinism and vast cosmic forces sweeping us along, over which we have no control. Instead of seeing beneath the great world empires and universal states, cast up by the convulsions of a dying civilization, the unity of mankind, we let ourselves be swept into the jumbled promiscuity of a cultural melting pot where almost all our distinctive differences are boiled away, and we sink into the amorphous eclecticism of a diluted, cultureless soup. Instead of an active martyrdom, attempting what lies even beyond the line of duty, we shrink away from duty itself, and even question its existence.

According to Toynbee, this is especially likely to happen to the thinkers and teachers whose duty it is to carry on the most crucially important of all cultural functions, the preservation in a clear and articulate state of the overarching purpose of the culture, and the principles on which it rests. When the intellectuals betray this vital function and, instead of preserving and defending the truth that is known, spend their precious time and energy in attacking truth and even the possibility of knowledge, this is the most dangerous form of sabotage. Then all becomes dim and unclear. The sharp outlines of principle and purpose give way to eclectic, philosophic syntheses, and religious syncretism. Different principles and different Gods become hyphenated together, and joined with the implacable advance of a rising secularism.

According to Toynbee, the great betrayal of the Western intellectuals, *la trahison des clercs,* cannot be identified with that recent and still continuing surrender of the principles of liberalism, to which Benda has called attention. This is only a late symptom of a much earlier betrayal which began during the Middle Ages and reached its first climax in the fifteenth and sixteenth centuries. As Toynbee says, 'The truancy which has given this latest exhibition of itself was set on foot, centuries earlier, when the "clerks" repudiated their clerical origin by trying to shift the rising edifice of our Western Christian Civilization from a religious to a secular basis. This was the original act of *hubris* which is being requited in our day by an *ate* that has been accumulating for centuries at compound interest.' (*A Study of History,* Oxford, 1947, pp. 443-4.)

It was this dilution of clear-cut Catholic principles by secular trends of thought, beginning with the fatal decision of Gregory VII on investiture, that led papal policy away from the goal of establishing a universal republic of Christendom into the channels of power politics, which led it to stifle the Conciliar movement of the fifteenth century, which brought forth the bitter nationalistic divisions of Reformation times, the pagan doctrine of the divine right of kings, and that pagan worship of the nation state which now is leading us to destruction.

I take it that we as a group are ready to agree with Toynbee that the only hope for our tottering culture is a return to the original ideal of a universal Republic of Christendom, a union of nations preserving their cultural diversities, but voluntarily accepting the guidance of Christian principles, or at least of philosophical principles reconcilable with Christianship. Just as the Church alone was capable of leading men at the time of the fall of the Roman Empire, and of guiding them in the foundation of a new civilization of Western Christendom, so is it today. Having failed in its first attempt, once again the Church is being given perhaps a second and last opportunity. Swayed by a sense of desperate urgency, great masses of men are looking for definite leadership. This is true even of trained scientific minds justifiably terrified by the present prospects of uncontrolled technology. Will the Church be able to meet this urgent and imperative need? Or will it fail again? Surely the prospects are not too hopeful.

The largest Christian body has inherited intact the full content of Christian thought, devotion, and liturgy. But at the same time it has also inherited something of that inflexible *hubris* which called forth the bitter reaction of the Renaissance and Reformation, thus shattering the world of Christendom and bringing upon us our time of troubles. Clinging rigidly not only to the basic principles of Christian philosophy and theology but to the now obsolete and antiquated techniques by which these principles were once applied to situations having little in common with those we face today, this august body has cut itself off both from what is bad and from what is good in modern life. Blindly adhering to certain incidental doctrines in its own tradition, it has rejected the light of modern science in anthropology, history, and Biblical research, and has allowed itself in these fields to fall into a position resembling that of the most antirational fundamentalism. Inflexibly maintaining social and political attitudes which may have been appropriate in dealing with princes and potentates in the era of feudal economy, it has in fact opposed almost all modern, liberal, democratic movements, in spite of enlightened statements in encyclicals.

Much as we may respect this great organization as in some way representing our parent body in a peculiar frozen state, we can have little hope, on the basis of the record, that it will give us any fruitful guidance in meeting the novel problems with which modern industrialism and democracy have confronted us. As Toynbee points out, this is an almost invariable sequence in history. The group or institution which successfully meets one challenge becomes intoxicated with victory, and holds itself aloof from new challenges, which have to be met, in so far as they are met at all, by some dark horse. Where is this dark horse to be found?

There are, of course, the innumerable Protestant sects. Some of them are certainly in a more flexible and, therefore, a more favorable position. The difficulty here lies at the opposite extreme. In their justifiable rebellion against autocracy and other abuses in the parent body, they have often become blind to certain essential elements in the Christian heritage which they have confused with accidents. Focusing on certain partial phases of this rich heritage, they have sometimes blown these to such monstrous proportions as to verge on heresy, which must be defined, of course, as a loss of balance in mistaking a part for the whole. If the Romans have unfortunately treasured and adored bathwater with the baby, the Protestants have unfortunately often thrown out the baby with the bath.

In these respects the Anglican Communion is at the present time in a unique position. It has neither thrown out any essential principle or element in the Catholic heritage, nor has it distrusted the masses and frozen itself into a regimented autocracy. If I were forced to choose a single phrase to represent its position at the present time, I should say that what it stands for is a democratic Catholicism, ready to accept and interpret all the genuine facts of science in the light of sound Catholic principles, and ready to give guidance, based on these same principles, in the attempt to establish a democratic Christendom.

Will the Church be able to respond to this challenge? I do not know. There are grave difficulties in the way. Democracy is easy to talk about, but like other precious things there is a price to pay. Even at the secular level we know that this price is the price of education. Secular democracy demands the education of the masses in natural knowledge. Religious democracy demands the education of the masses in both natural and supernatural knowledge, which is both theology and philosophy. This is not an easy task. The Church today is filled with a vast, uninformed membership teeming with secular notions derived from our decaying culture, and utterly irreconcilable with Catholicism, though widely confused with it. The result is a blurring of sharp outline and principle, which some sectarian apologists, confusing it with a virtue, have called 'the genius of Anglicanism.'

I do not regard intellectual vagueness and compromise as a virtue. I think that intellectual or moral flexibility, as it is sometimes called—that is, the capacity to adapt firmly held principles to new situations by both thought and action—is a most important virtue. But this virtue of flexibility cannot be identified with the lack of clear-cut principles. It is precisely a vague and slipshod way of thought which is likely to confuse its own subjective opinions with the independent truth, and thus to cling with stubborn tenacity to antiquated methods and formulae. On the other hand, it is clear insight into fixed first principles which alone enables us to meet the ever-changing contingencies of the concrete situation with a firm and guided flexibility. The third-rate navigator who has learned a certain routine can find his position under normal conditions as well as the expert can. But in an emergency, when something breaks, under novel conditions, he will be helpless. Here we need a man who knows something of astronomy and the basic principles of the sciences.

Similarly the Church cannot meet the unprecedented challenges of our time without a sharp and clear insight into first principles, both philosophical and theological.

In my opinion, the basic principles of the Catholic Faith to which the Anglican Communion is committed are most clearly, sharply, and exhaustively expressed first of all in that realistic philosophy which was founded by the Greeks, enormously deepened, extended, and refined by its contact with Christianity in the Middle Ages, and further refined and developed down to the present time; and second, in the great medieval compendia of theology, particularly the *Summa Theologica,* which have also been deepened and perfected by both Roman and Anglican elucidation, application, and commentary.

This perennial philosophy is not accurately expressed by the term 'Thomism.' First of all we need not agree with papal authority and with those Protestant apologists who so effectively spread this papal opinion. I cannot believe that a tradition to which Plato, Aristotle, Augustine, Averroes, Avicenna, Aquinas, Cajetan, Hooker, and countless other keen minds have contributed throughout the whole of our Western history is to be regarded as the property of a single Christian sect. Secondly, there are certain aspects of the Thomistic synthesis which, it is now clear, require radical revision. This is, of course, true of cosmological hypotheses connected with medieval science which are far removed from first principles. It is also true of certain theories in the field of social philosophy which are not so far removed. Finally, I find it quite possible to believe that this great body of philosophical and theological doctrine will be further deepened and extended by painstaking toil and labor in the future, as it has already been deepened and extended in the past.

The many works which have been heralded as revolutionary novelties and original achievements of the first magnitude in recent times have on the whole disappointed me. I have often sat down to read such works with a real thrill of expectation only to find that their supposed originality consisted either in an appalling ignorance of what has been achieved in the past, in tearing some truth from its context and blowing it up to such gigantic proportions that it can hardly be recognized, or in definite mistakes which might be remedied by a deeper study of philosophy and theology. So I have returned to the classic texts of these sciences, though I know that should I devote all the remaining days and nights of my life to their study I should never succeed in mastering the little that has already been learned.

This of course is not the time or place for any attempt on my part to expound even one such basic doctrine with precision. Nevertheless, I am going to attempt a cataloguing of these basic doctrines for the sake of possibly clarifying discussion. Here then is a list of what I take to be the cardinal theses of realistic philosophy and Catholic theology which, it would seem to me, we are all under obligation to understand and defend to the best of our ability.

No doubt some of you will question the inclusion of philosophical doctrines in this list. Is this not due perhaps to some professional bias on the part of the author? If this were only true, we should be free from heavy burdens of prolonged reflection and tedious debate. Unfortunately, it is not true. Men cannot think without the use of basic categories, and the critical use of basic categories is philosophy. A thoughtless theology with no logos is a contradiction, an impossibility for man.

I shall not elaborate this point any further beyond noting the fact that certain types of philosophy, including most of those which are currently influential—positivism, naturalism, and idealistic pantheism—are radically inconsistent and irreconcilable with Christianity. This indicates plainly enough that in defending theological principles one is also making certain philosophical assumptions, even though he may not be clearly aware of them. As a matter of fact, many so-called theological differences are rather philosophical than theological, and we do not escape from this humiliating situation by ignoring it. So I shall begin with a skeleton list of those realistic doctrines which it seems to me are presupposed by the Christian Faith.

Epithets and tags are of course always misleading and unfortunate. It would be nicer, of course, if we could simply refer to certain truths of philosophy which are presupposed by the truths of religion. This I think would be a more accurate mode of reference. But in the present chaotic state of this discipline, where there are almost as many divergent concepts of philosophy as there are individual philosophers, this also would be misunderstood and confused with dogmatism. So I am choosing the epithet *realism* as the least objectionable, partly because of historical associations, and partly because what it suggests is something evident and close to the common insight of common men, which is always true of the best philosophy.

Here then are three doctrines that must lie at the root of any realistic mode of thought, one concerning the world we inhabit, the second concerning our knowledge of this world, and the third concerning the direction of human conduct. I shall not be able to develop the implications of these theses very far, but shall restrict myself to a bare minimum of explanatory comment. I shall omit all reference to natural theology, postponing this to the succeeding section on theology.

1. The world is made up of contingent, substantial entities existing in an order of real relations, which is independent of human opinion and desire.

This is an assertion of pluralistic realism. A substantial entity is one which exists in itself, and not as an accident in something formally distinct from itself, as the skin color or the relation 'son of' in an individual man.

Real relations, as opposed to mere mental acts of comparison, are accidents, and thus require a plurality of substances in which they inhere.

A substance is contingent if it may either be or not be, or in technical language if its essence is distinct from its existence. Anything whose nonexistence may be thought without contradiction is contingent.

This thesis implies a rejection of pantheistic monism, which is incompatible not only with Christianity because of its denial of the transcendence of God, but with the facts of experience as well, because of its denial of real substances and relations.

The evidence of experience also clearly indicates that both material being, which is individual and quantitative, and mental being, which is universal and nonquantitative, exist in the world. Hence both materialism, which reduces being to material being, and idealism, which reduces being to mental being, are rejected. This is also in harmony with the central Christian doctrine of the Incarnation, which surely implies the existence of physical flesh or matter, as well as that of mental consciousness and awareness.

2. These real substances, accidents, and relations can be known by the human mind as they are in themselves.

This thesis is an assertion of epistemological realism or rationalism. Knowledge is not the making or constructing of any new material entity. It is rather the immaterial assimilation of something determinate already in existence. The physicist can understand the properties of a vapor without being physically vaporized. The geologist can understand the nature of a rock without becoming petrified.

Physically man is a frail and insignificant creature crawling about the surface of a minor satellite of a minor star. Physical forces may easily annihilate him. But he alone in this vast panoply of nature is able to lift all these things, as well as himself, into that immaterial presence before the mind which we call consciousness or awareness. Noetically or intentionally man is all things—a microcosm, including everything from the stellar galaxies to the atomic nuclei, within the range of his immaterial awareness. This is the ultimate source of human freedom and dignity, and it is in this sense alone, as St. Augustine pointed out, that we can understand the Christian dogma that man is made in the image of God.

3. Such knowledge, especially that treating of human nature, can provide us with immutable principles for the free guidance of human action, both individual and social.

This thesis is an assertion of ethical realism, the existence of a real good and evil embedded in the nature of things and subject to human choice, altogether independent of any human opinion or tyrannical decree. To some degree, these have always been known by men and have been expressed in the ancient concept of the law of nature, or the moral law. Note that the thesis asserts only that there is such a law, and that men can know it. There is no assertion that man must follow it, nor that once having broken it, he is able to follow it by his own efforts alone.

Man is a finite entity requiring further accidental being, namely action, for the realization of the nature with which he has been endowed. This action must be social or co-operative. The initial tendency to such action is physically inherent in every individual. But it cannot be adequately fulfilled unless it is directed by rational understanding of human nature, and of that universal pattern of action which is required by this nature for its perfection. This universal pattern of action is the law of nature, or the moral law. As founded on the nature of man as such, it is immutable. But since man must act as an individual in varying circumstances, the universal principles of natural law require further determinations made by free choice to meet ever-changing situations.

Here then are three germinal theses of philosophy from which all else that is sound may be developed with the aid of acute empirical observation: in metaphysics the assertion of a plurality of substances which exist independent of our thought and desire, *realism;* in epistemology, the assertion of the fact of human knowledge, *rationalism;* in practical philosophy, the assertion of a real good and evil ingrained in the nature of things, *the law of nature.* Realism, rationalism, and the law of nature are three distinct but inseparable components of the central core of Western philosophy, I should say of any sound philosophy. I recommend them to your attention.

Of course the fundamental reason for believing in these principles is that they can be seen to be true, and will stand up under the careful scrutiny of the individual intellect. But there are certain supporting reasons that I believe should have a certain weight with us. In the first place, these theses are in definite accord with dogmas of the faith. As we have pointed out, Christianity cannot be reconciled with any monistic pantheism which must deny the transcendence of God. Thus in the Nicene Creed we do not say maker of one thing, or maker of one common field of experience, but 'maker of all things visible and invisible,' i.e. material and immaterial, physical and mental.

As to the peculiar, rational dignity of man, we are told that man was made in the image of God (a purely immaterial, omniscient being); we are ordered to love God with all our heart, and all our soul, and all our mind; and finally our human nature has been taken over by God himself in the Incarnation.

As to the moral law and the freedom of man, we need only remember that the Christian revelation includes commands, to be carried out by man in a responsible manner. One does not issue commands to unconscious entities, nor does one hold them responsible. One simply manipulates them. Christianity cannot be reconciled with any philosophy which denies the freedom of man both before and after the fall, and a natural knowledge of good and evil. Hence I think it is fair to say that, more than any other philosophical alternative yet developed in the history of Western thought, realism is in precise accord with the content of Christian Revelation.

In the second place we must give a certain weight to the fact that this philosophy has been adopted, cultivated, and refined by keen minds from the fifth century B.C. right down to the present day. It is fair to say that it has been tested by more great minds for a longer period in more different cultural settings than any that is at present available to us.

Finally, in the third place, it is in agreement with the basic insights of the common man. I know that there are those who would hold this to be a disadvantage rather than an advantage, and who glory in their defiance of what they call common sense. But I cannot agree. If the human rational faculty is so distorted as to lead us basically astray in our most fundamental apprehensions, then it seems to me there is little hope for any individual philosopher or even a school of philosophy to set us straight. The whole enterprise had better be abandoned. If it is basically sound, then its primary insights should be respected. Surely these agree with the basic theses of realism, for the common man knows that he exists in a pluralistic universe, which is sustained by causes independent of his opinions, his desires, and even his existence. He recognizes that knowledge is a fact, and respects it as a guide for conduct. When he is sick, he goes to a doctor.

Realistic philosophy does respect these insights and maintains a vital contact with them. It does not attempt to break them down, but rather to clarify them, to refine them, and to protect them by rational argument and deduction against attacks to which they are very susceptible when left in a vague and undeveloped form. In fact, this philosophy is best understood as a healing therapy for the common intellect of the common man, a means of preserving mental sanity and health. So the jibe that realism is nothing but common sense with a few refinements is to be accepted. What is the highest cultural achievement but nature with a few refinements? This is a point in its favor.

But it is now time to turn to theology. Here I must be more brief. I shall first of all list the basic propositions in natural theology to which I believe we are committed, and then those in revealed theology.

First, of course, there are the arguments for the existence of God. The ontological argument, never influential until it was taken up by Descartes and his followers, must be rejected by any realist, since it makes an illicit passage from mental to extramental being. Given the background of a realistic analysis of natural change, the causal arguments, based upon observed *empirical* facts, must be accepted. For example, if natural substances are all contingent and have been brought into being, then they must have been brought into being by an ultimate, first cause, which is noncontingent, or whose essence is existence. In order to understand and classify these arguments, one must study them in their classical formulations. The well-known Kantian version of the arguments is quite accurate.

From the results of these demonstrations, a large number of consequences may be rigorously deduced; for example, that God is being, that His essence is existence, and that He, therefore, exists necessarily. There is no time to go through the arguments. I shall merely list the attributes which realistic philosophy claims to be able to demonstrate.

These are absolute simplicity, because composition involves contingency; transcendence, because a simple being cannot be mixed to form any composite whole; infinity, because no positive perfection or degree of perfection is excluded by being; perfect activity, because unactualized potency is a limitation or imperfection of being; immutability, because change is the passage from potency to act; eternity, because time cannot measure being which perfectly possesses its existence all at once without succession; immateriality, because matter is potential and imperfect; intelligence, because to be without material limitation is to understand; will, because God is both active and intelligent, and action united with intelligence is will; personality, because a person is a rational substance; freedom, because He is aware of possibilities and capable of choosing among them; and finally the creator of the world not by any necessary emanation but by a free act of choice, neither indeterminate caprice nor the result of any moral necessity.

These are some of the consequences that may be deduced without any overt appeal to faith from the first demonstrations. I find that Anglicans are apt to be surprised at what they regard as these excessive claims. It may be that Christianity is less unreasonable than they are inclined to suppose.

I shall be forced to be even briefer in dealing with the field of dogmatic theology, not because of any desire to slight it, but rather from sheer limitation of time, and a sense that the more important issues now dividing members of the Church tend to lie in these fields. Of course, one need not be a Christian to hold all the foregoing doctrines. As a matter of fact, most of them have been held by non-Christian philosophers of different civilizations, for example by Plato and Aristotle. What we have stated is not religion at all. It is merely sound philosophy. Nevertheless, religious revelation presupposes knowledge of this kind.

When we meet someone for the first time of whose existence we have been hitherto completely ignorant, we do not say that he has *revealed* himself to us. Revelation is not discovery. But if someone concerning whom we have only a general knowledge in terms of his effects—that he has held such and such an office, for instance, that he has been responsible for this or that—if he suddenly communicates to us something of his inner life and his personal attitude toward us, then we speak of this as a revelation or disclosure. To know that something is hidden from us is to know incompletely, but it is to know.

Our common insight is dimly aware of the fact that man did not bring himself into existence, that the ordered cosmos has a higher cause. Only the fool is blind to this. The conclusions of natural theology, which we have just listed, are merely a clarification and articulation of this dim knowledge of the *Deus absconditus* which is common to mankind. But this knowledge, even when carefully formulated and refined, gives us only a public knowledge of the first cause through His various effects. It tells us nothing of His inner, private life, so to speak, and of His personal attitude toward us. The content of dogmatic theology which is summarized in the Creeds is such a revelation made by the eruption of God Himself into the matter and flesh of human history.

It is, of course, divided into three distinct but inseparable parts. The first concerns the inner life of God Himself—the doc-

trine of the Trinity. The second concerns the revelation of His
personal attitude and intentions toward us through an actual
human life lived by Him—the central doctrine of the Incarnation
and its implications. The third concerns the sacramental and
corporate extension of this life in history—the doctrine of the
Church and its implications. I shall restrict my brief remarks to
the third, on the ground that the issues with which we are
chiefly concerned lie chiefly in this field rather than the first two.

Like any human institution, the Church is founded on a common understanding of a common good, in this case the redemption of man from disorder and sin, and a love of this common
good. But for the Christian, the Church is distinguished from all
other institutions and groups by the fact that it was founded by
God in His incarnate life, and is continuously sustained and
strengthened by the enduring presence of this very life within it.

Of course, as the source of all being, God is always present
everywhere, but not in a manner which we can directly understand and appreciate. He is eternal; we are temporal. He is immaterial; we are material. The gulf is too great. The limitations
of our nature make it impossible for us to come into any warm
and living relationship with such a being. In order that we might
enjoy such a relationship God had to enter into the world of
matter, taking upon Himself all the limitations of human flesh,
and living a finite human life in *forma servi*. In this way, He
could become sensibly and physically present to us, and could
exert an effect upon the material events of human history without interfering with human freedom, by appealing to us and act-
ing upon us as a man among men.

The impact of this eruption was profound. An actual human
life was lived and finished. The Church was founded. If this had
been only a human life, it would have been remembered for
some time. Its effects, ever widening like the ripples from a
splash, would have gradually faded away, as they merged with
the other ripples of a common civilization. Finally, when the
civilization disintegrated, it would have passed into oblivion.
But God had other means at His disposal. Through the sacraments, this life once lived was preserved and maintained within
the Church, to be shared and corporately extended through on-

coming generations. Thus it has not been forgotten and has not faded away. Of all the manifold organizations and institutions of the Hellenic World, the Church alone survived the cataclysmic fall of the Hellenic culture.

This unique power and strength must have some explanation. For the Christian, it is explained by the sacramental presence of divine life in the Church. In this way, we are not only present to Him, which is always the case, but He becomes present to us under physical forms which we can sensibly appreciate and understand. It is this divine life, sacramentally shared by the members, which reclarifies the common understanding, rekindles the common aspiration, and binds them together in one common body, bringing forth that peculiar, corporate vitality which history records.

Hence the extraordinary tenacity with which Christians have clung, and must cling, to the sacraments. For through them they are brought into living contact, so far as they are able to bear it, with something immune to time and the ever-threatening collapse of civilization. Any attempt to break the sacramental continuity of the Church, to view the sacraments humanistically as mnemonic devices, or to interpret them subjectively as valid only so far as they produce edifying thoughts and feelings in the recipients must be resisted as an attempt to secularize the Church, and to reduce it to the level of ordinary human institutions. The Christian must hold that there is a real presence quite distinct from any purely psychic presence in his thought, and that the sacrament works *ex opere operato* whatever he may be thinking or feeling. What is now generally referred to as the 'spiritual' way of understanding the sacraments as a matter of fact is a mode of subjectivism and individualism quite inconsistent with Christian realism, and with that corporate character of the liturgy which is one of its primary manifestations.

History shows us all too clearly what finally happens to human institutions, even to those that are noblest and best. Eventually they become the servants of human pride and lethargy, and sink into the dust. God knows we see this happening in every branch of the Church, including our own. We see it, I think, especially in those 'spiritual' modes of interpreting the liturgy as a helpful and comforting escape from trouble, which was correctly and pungently diagnosed first of all by Kingsley, long before Marx, as an opiate of the people. Instead of the sacrifice of human aspiration, pride, and libido, the complete and voluntary abandonment of soul and body to the service of God, religion then becomes inverted into a supposed sacrifice of God to the service of human libido.

It is this fearful misunderstanding and misuse of the sacraments that calls forth a bitter revulsion from the keenest pagan minds, and from our own as well. How can any honest and discerning person watch the Church at the present time being used in every one of its sects and branches to spread a false feeling of righteousness and security, and thus to bolster up the injustices and enormities of a sick civilization without a profound sense of corruption, futility, and frustration? *Corruptio melioris pejor*. What then is the remedy?

Surely not to throw away what is being corrupted and misused by us. This would be merely to cure the disease by cutting ourselves off from the source of life, a further manifestation of subjective pride. The only remedy is a revival of faith, and that keen sense of transcendent reality which genuine faith always brings. What distinguishes the Church from all other institutions is not organization, not co-operative activity, not power, not exalted purposes and ideas, not high-minded men, not nice people. All of these have been possessed by innumerable other institutions in other civilizations as well as our own, and history shows us all too clearly that they are no match for human pride and greed.

The distinguishing mark of the Church is the divine life that lives sacramentally within her, offering to men not rest-in-self through escapism but self-sacrifice through that transfiguration of material life here and now which Toynbee holds out as the only hope for our disintegrating culture. This sacramental life does not work automatically or magically, but it lives and works. Hence it seems to me that it is our duty to resist any tendency to dilute or to water down the realistic sacramental doctrine and practice of the Church so sedulously guarded in the past by our communion.

This great treasure of sacramental devotion, together with its guiding principles, has been given to the Anglican communion to be voluntarily guarded without autocratic safeguards, to be used in meeting the democratic challenges of the modern world, and to be bestowed upon free peoples, without removing their freedom by regimentation. We do not lock up this treasure in great fortresses. We try to protect it by insight and intelligence rather than by power and force. We are ready to bestow it upon anyone who is ready to receive it voluntarily, with understanding of what he is doing. But readiness for union, real generosity, implies that we have something to give. We do not magnify our ultimate contribution to Christian unity by allowing our treasure to evaporate and to be whittled away.

The central core of this treasure that has been bestowed upon us is the divine sacramental life in the body of the Church with its doctrinal basis. This is inextricably intertwined with the rest of dogmatic theology, the dogmas of the Trinity and the Incarnation. This in turn presupposes that knowledge of the *Deus absconditus* which is contained in natural theology. This finally presupposes the three basic truths of realistic philosophy: that we inhabit a pluralistic universe of contingent substances not dependent upon us for their existence, realism; that we can know these things as they are in themselves, rationalism; and finally that we can know the moral law, and can direct our action in accordance therewith.

It is, of course, the privilege of scholars in the Church further to supplement and extend this great body of truth. But their primary duty, as I see it, is to keep its outlines sharp and clear, to guard it against vagueness, eclectic confusion, and secular adulteration, and finally to focus its light upon the unprecedented problems of contemporary life which must be soon met with the resolution of high purpose, if our sick culture is to be saved from chaos and destruction.

Theology and Philosophy: a Mediating View

BY GEORGE F. THOMAS

Q

One of the most important intellectual tasks of our time is to define more clearly the relation between theology and philosophy. In the Middle Ages theology tended to subordinate philosophy to herself, making it a mere 'handmaid' in the service of the 'queen of the sciences.' With the Renaissance, philosophy declared its independence and threw off the authority of the Christian revelation as expressed in the theology of the Church. By the eighteenth century the tables had been completely turned: theology was on the defensive against the attacks of a militant philosophy whose watchword was 'natural religion.' Early in the nineteenth century the ablest philosophers recognized that the attempt to construct a religion by reason without benefit of revelation was a failure. German Idealism, therefore, sought to develop a theory of religion that would do justice to historical religion and the religious consciousness. But it reduced Christianity to the terms of its own monistic philosophy and distorted it at points beyond recognition. The attack upon this Idealism by Kierkegaard was not widely noticed in his time. But the insistence by Ritschl, Harnack, and other Liberals upon the historical basis of Christianity and their repudiation of every alliance of theology with Greek or modern metaphysics had a strong effect. The divorce of theology from philosophy begun by them has been completed in our time by Karl Barth, who has insisted that the Word of God is the sole source of theology.

The consequences of this break have been tragic. Though philosophy had been subordinated to theology in the Middle Ages and theology had been progressively subordinated to philosophy in the Modern Age, each took the other seriously and tried to come to terms with it. In our day, however, each tends to go its own way in disregard of the other, and there is a real danger that fruitful interaction between them will cease. Philosophy has, to a large extent, lost interest in the problems of religious belief, as the dearth of good American books on the philosophy of religion since before the First World War shows. It has either abandoned metaphysics altogether, as in Logical Positivism, or fallen under the spell of science and accepted Naturalism as the last word. Theology has in Barthian circles abandoned philosophy as a pretentious but futile product of the sin of pride, and has limited itself to the restatement of the content of the Church's preaching without attempting to relate it to modern thought and culture.

Fortunately, the tradition of Theism, which arose in the West from the synthesis of Greek philosophy and Christian faith, has never been lost from modern philosophy and continues to have some influence in America. Though it is weak in the larger university departments of philosophy in comparison with Naturalism, it continues to make itself heard there, and it is still dominant in seminary circles. Fortunately, too, there are many theologians who have refused to follow the lead of either Ritschl or Barth in repudiating philosophy. Natural theology has been well established in Roman Catholic thought since the time of St. Thomas; it has had many well known representatives among Anglicans and Presbyterians in Britain; and Liberal Protestant thinkers in America have given it much attention. Moreover, the attempt to expel Christian apologetics from theology has not been wholly successful even in Continental theology, as the example of Brunner shows, and it has failed to appeal to more than a minority of the theologians of Britain and America. Thus, the divorce of theology from philosophy is far from final. The issue is still an open one.

NATURAL THEOLOGY

If we are to think clearly about the relation of theology to philosophy, we must distinguish between three kinds of theology: natural or philosophical theology; systematic or revealed theology; and apologetics. As we shall be concerned with the first two, it is necessary to give a broad definition of each of them. Natural or philosophical theology does not start from the presuppositions of any historical religion but seeks to draw conclusions about God and the world from evidence available to all alike. Systematic or revealed theology, on the other hand, uses reason to develop the meaning and implications of the Christian revelation which has been accepted by faith. We shall deal first with natural or philosophical theology, because it has recently been rejected altogether by some and regarded as of little importance by other Protestant theologians of the continent of Europe.

The views of Emil Brunner in his *Revelation and Reason* will will help us to understand this negative attitude. First, Brunner holds that the traditional arguments for the existence of God in themselves 'possess considerable, and indeed convincing, cogency,' but that there is 'no court of appeal which—from the outside, as it were—can establish the rightness or wrongness of the proofs.' The result is that 'many, but by no means the majority, or even all who have been competent to deal with the problem, regard the proofs for the existence of God as verifiable. . . It would seem, therefore, that the acceptance or rejection of the proofs for the existence of God must involve other elements besides rational ones.' (pp. 339-40) Second, 'faith has no interest in them' because 'the way in which the divine revelation produces the certainty of faith is quite different from that of proof, and it is completely independent of the success or failure of the process of proof.' (p. 340) Third, 'The content of the knowledge "secured" by these proofs is something quite different from the content of the knowledge of faith. The "God" of the proofs . . . is not the Living God of faith, but an intellectual abstraction, an "Idea," an "Absolute," a "Highest," etc.' (p. 341) Thus, Brunner holds that faith has no concern with the proofs of natural theology, that they do not produce conviction where there is not a predisposition to accept them, and that they do not prove the existence of the Living God of religion. Finally, he thinks that they have been developed under the strong influence of the Christian faith and cannot stand apart from it. 'Where they are supported by the Christian tradition,' he says, 'the abstract idea which they attain is related to the Christian idea of God in some way or another; but where the Christian basis disappears they lose not only their convincing power, but also their Christian theistic content.' (p. 348)

At first sight these criticisms appear to be devastating, but actually they point to limitations of natural theology without destroying its value. (1) The fact that many do not accept the proofs of the existence of God as valid does suggest that other than rational factors are usually involved in the acceptance or rejection of them. But these factors have nothing to do with the validity or invalidity of the proofs themselves. (2) The fact that faith often 'takes no interest in them' because it depends upon revelation rather than argument is also irrelevant to the question of their validity. The proofs were not designed primarily to appeal to men of faith but to convince men without faith, on the one hand, and to strengthen the faith of those assailed by doubts, on the other. (3) It is true that the knowledge gained from the proofs is not knowledge of the Living God of faith in the sense of a direct encounter with Him in experience. It is knowledge about God rather than direct knowledge of God. The latter must come from a personal experience of His reality. Nevertheless, it is misleading to say that the knowledge about God offered by the proofs is nothing more than an 'intellectual abstraction.' All philosophical knowledge, of course, is expressed in abstract conceptual terms, but the object or content of such knowledge may be a concrete personal Being. (4) Finally, the fact that the proofs of natural theology have been more convincing when the Christian faith has been strong does not mean that they are mere rationalizations of that faith. For the beginnings of these proofs, especially the cosmological and teleological ones, are to be found in Plato and Aristotle long before Christ. And, though

their development as we know them was undoubtedly influenced
by the Christian faith, they are based upon evidence drawn from
other sources, as we shall see.

In an earlier book, Brunner manifests a greater appreciation of
the function and value of natural theology. In criticizing the exclusive claims made by Barth for the 'special' revelation in the
Bible, he insists upon the reality of the 'general' revelation of
God in nature, conscience, and history. Moreover, there is in
man a capacity to respond to this revelation of God, a capacity
due to the fact that the form of the 'image of God' in him has
not been lost as a result of sin. The 'proofs' of the existence of
God, he suggests, should be regarded as indications derived from
this general revelation rather than as demonstrations, and their
value is limited in that they are inadequate to bring man
knowledge of the true God and have not prevented him from
setting up idols of his own imagination. Thus, Brunner asserts
the desirability of natural theology as an attempt to interpret
general revelation, while insisting upon its limitations and perversions as it has actually been used by man.

This, it seems to me, is a sounder way of viewing the attain-
ments of natural theology. The traditional 'proofs' and their
modern variants cannot prove the existence of the God of Christianity. Men's knowledge of the God of love and mercy has come
through a historical revelation rather than a rational demonstration. The 'God of the philosophers,' as Pascal said, is not the
'God of Abraham, Isaac, and Jacob." For this reason the Christian must demur at the excessive claims of rationalistic representatives of natural theology like St. Thomas. At the end of
each of his 'proofs' of God in the *Summa Theologica*, St. Thomas
says of the First Mover or First Cause he has attempted to
demonstrate that 'this we understand' or 'everyone understands
to be God.' This is misleading, to say the least. The God of
Christianity is doubtless Prime Mover and First Cause of the
world, but He is far more than that. He is also more than the
Highest Being of the fourth or the Intelligent Agent of the fifth
proof of St. Thomas.[1] Philosophical theism should never claim
to do more than it can do. From data derived from our experience of nature the God of love and mercy manifested in

Christ cannot be inferred. Even the moral argument that Kant substituted for the traditional proofs of St. Thomas falls short of that high theme.

Indeed, it is dubious whether the existence of God in any religious sense of the term can be proved without appealing to religious experience. The identification of the metaphysical First Principle demonstrated by the traditional proofs with a God who can be worshipped is meaningless to those without any experience of God. This means that we must refuse to follow the lead of those natural theologians from St. Thomas to F. R. Tennant who attempt to prove the existence of God from data of the senses without recourse to religious experience. These theologians have doubtless been motivated by the laudable desire to use a 'scientific' method which unbelievers, distrustful of religious experience as 'subjective,' will accept. But they are surely wrong in surrendering the most convincing evidence of God's existence, the fact that men have had personal experience of Him. At this point Christian Platonists, mystics, and simple believers have been on firmer ground than Aristotelians like St. Thomas and Empiricists like Tennant, for they have recognized that men are convinced of the existence of a spiritual, super-sensible Reality primarily by a direct intuitive apprehension rather than by an inference from sense data.

It is not, however, a case of either/or, but of both/and. We do not know God indirectly alone, through rational inference from His effects in the Creation; nor do we know Him directly alone, through religious experience and intuition. We know Him both indirectly and directly. H. H. Farmer, in his little book *Towards Belief in God,* has argued that the really convincing—or, as he puts it rather misleadingly, 'coercive'—argument for the existence of the God of Theism is experience of Him as the transcendent, holy Source of the absolute demands laid upon our wills and of the final succour that meets our deepest need.[2] But he believes also that a number of 'confirmatory' or supporting arguments are suggested to us by reflection upon the general course of human experience, e.g. the moral life, the appreciation of beauty, and the nature of the evolutionary process.[3] None of these arguments, he thinks, 'demonstrates' the existence of God; none of them produces 'certainty.' But when they are taken together, they establish the probability of Theism as a more adequate explanation of all the facts than any other philosophy. Thus a reasoned belief in God is the result of religious experience confirmed by philosophical reflection.

The difference between this approach to natural theology and that of St. Thomas is striking. For one thing, it is recognized that the existence of God cannot be conclusively proved by any one proof, but that the proof is a cumulative one in which strands of evidence from various sources are woven together. Careful analysis of nature by an unbiased mind can and does suggest a cosmic Mind as the Source of its order, its beauty, and its evolution up to man. Reflection on the absolute moral imperatives with which the will of man is confronted carries us further and indicates a cosmic Will characterized by goodness. These and other lines of reflection give rise to Theism as a philosophical hypothesis concerning the Ground of the natural and moral order. When religious experience is also taken into account, the probability of this hypothesis is greatly increased and to the deeply religious person it passes into certitude. Whether religious experience is taken into account at the beginning of this process of reflection, as in Farmer's argument, or comes in only at the end, as in the arguments of some others, is a secondary matter. What is important is that it can be and has been confirmed and supported by a cumulative argument that takes into account many kinds of facts.

In short, natural theology has become empirical rather than rationalistic and consequently is now more modest in its claims. The greatest natural theologians like Archbishop Temple do not make excessive claims for natural theology. In his *Nature, Man and God*, Temple restates and combines the cosmological and moral arguments: the emergence of human mind and goodness in the cosmic process is intelligible only if we postulate a divine Mind and Goodness immanent in that process but also transcendent to it.[4] But he also insists that religious experience and revelation provide part of the data which should be considered by natural theology.[5] Thus, natural theology using an empirical approach is justified and its data are extended. At the same time, as we shall see, Temple shows that natural religion or theology points beyond itself to a special historical revelation of God.[6]

Thus, the work of recent philosophers like Farmer and Temple has indicated that natural theology may be empirical in its method and that it may be able to prove the existence of God with a high degree of probability by means of a cumulative argument which includes data derived from religious experience as well as from nature. It is significantly different in all of these respects from the traditional natural theology of St. Thomas, which was rationalistic in its method (despite the beginning of the 'proofs' from facts of experience), claimed to produce certainty, depended upon a series of separate and independent proofs, and made no appeal to religious experience. The greater modesty of the claims of the empirical theology for reason and the wider range of evidence to which it appeals makes its arguments more complex but also more appealing to modern minds than those of the older rationalistic theology.

What are we to say, however, to the charge of Brunner that the witness of natural theology even in this empirical form is not an independent one but is simply an echo of the witness of faith? First, it is not true that it offers no independent witness. If there is a general revelation of God through nature, conscience, and history—as we should expect if God is the Creator of nature and the providential Governor of history—the attempt of reason to interpret that revelation may be expected to supplement as well as confirm what special revelation has to say to us. To deny the value of this general revelation out of jealousy for the special revelation in Christ, as Barth does, is to deny the common religious heritage of all men and thus to make impossible any point of contact with other religions than our own. Even more important, it is to close our eyes to the light that is all around us and to sin against the Holy Spirit which leads us into all truth. If the Christian doctrine of the Creation is true, the wisdom, power, and goodness of God are to be found in the course of nature and history as well as in the word that came to the prophets and apostles. Natural theology is simply the effort of thoughtful men to read the lessons that are to be found in the natural and moral orders and to show that both of these orders issue from a divine Source.

Second, even if natural theology were impossible or unconvincing without the stimulus of the Christian revelation, it would still have its value. Faith must be tested by confronting it with the facts of nature and human life. If these facts are found by reason to confirm it, it becomes more firmly established. Also, it becomes better understood in its implications and hence richer in its meaning. Moreover, these facts, if faced honestly and realistically, help to purify the faith of arbitrary, superstitious, and provincial elements.

Third, one of the main functions of natural theology is to prepare unbelievers for faith. As we have said, natural theology uses concepts that enable men only to know about God, and men must experience God before they can know Him as a living reality. But unless one holds with the mystics that knowledge through concepts completely distorts the object known, there is a place for such knowledge. It cannot produce faith in God, but it can produce the belief that His existence is probable. Something must happen to a man before this belief can become faith in the religious sense. Natural theology cannot make it happen. But it can prepare the way for it to happen.

Temple has pointed out that it is the need for deliverance from evil, especially from the sin of self-centeredness, that requires men to pass from natural religion or theology to revealed religion. For deliverance from sin requires that a man abandon and submit himself to that which can lift him out of himself, and natural theology 'cannot win him to worship.' 'It may assure him,' Temple says, 'that there is a God who both claims and deserves his worship; it may bid him to seek that God and the way to worship Him; but it cannot confront him with the God whom it describes. It can only discuss God; it cannot reveal Him. And for this reason the whole fabric of thought is liable to be laid in ruins by devastating doubt. For the existence of God is fully credible only if evil is being transmitted into good. . . Therefore, Natural Theology, which is indispensable as a source of interpretation and as a purge of superstition even for those who have received a true revelation, yet if left to itself, ends in a hunger which it cannot satisfy, and yet of which it must perish if no satisfaction is forthcoming.' [7]

This, it seems to me, is the right way to look at the strength and weakness of natural theology. Natural theology can 'discuss' God and show that His existence as Cosmic Mind and Goodness is probable, but it cannot 'confront him [man] with the God whom it describes.' It can build up the arch, but it cannot lay the keystone. Therefore, we should accept with gratitude all it can say to us, and at the same time we should recognize that it points beyond itself to the special revelation that fulfils it without destroying it.

REVEALED OR SYSTEMATIC THEOLOGY

The second type of theology is Revealed or Systematic Theology. It is called 'revealed,' of course, because it is based upon a special revelation of God in history, 'systematic' because it seeks to present the meaning of that revelation in a coherent and comprehensive way. It has also been called Dogmatic Theology, because in its traditional form it conceives of the revelation as consisting of dogmas that have been formulated once and for all by the Church. In this traditional form its distinctive characteristic has been its use of reason to elucidate, elaborate, and apply these dogmas which have been accepted without question by faith. As reason is thus subordinated to faith in dogmatic theology, philosophy becomes a mere 'handmaid' to theology.

1. As St. Thomas conceives revealed theology,[8] it is a science in that it sets forth with the help of reason and in an orderly way the meaning and implications of the faith. Like any other science, it derives conclusions by argument from its 'principles,' which are the 'articles of faith,' of the Church. These 'principles,' he admits, differ from those of other sciences in that they are not self-evident to reason. But they are more rather than less certain than those of other sciences, because they are derived from divine revelation, which is more trustworthy as a source of knowledge than fallible human reason. Therefore, theology is not only a science, it is also the noblest of the sciences and can condemn the conclusions of the other sciences when

they conflict with its own. It does not attempt to demonstrate its 'principles,' though some propositions can be demonstrated by natural theology; instead, it argues *from* its 'principles.' It can remove the objections of unbelievers to revelation, but it cannot prove to them that the articles of faith are true. Thus, the primary function of philosophy in revealed theology is the clarification of the meaning of the articles of faith and the deduction of their implications.

The reason for this limitation of the function of philosophy is to be found in part in St. Thomas' conception of revelation. Revelation, it seems, consists of the impression by God of images and ideas upon the minds of the prophets and apostles. It is truths or propositions that are thus revealed, and these can be and have been defined once and for all by the Church. The faith by which man apprehends these is based not upon knowledge that they are true but upon a volition of the will which moves the intellect to assent to them. Thus, both the method of revelation to prophets and apostles and the faith by which it is received by Christian believers are nonrational.

As a result of this sharp separation of revelation and faith from reason, the function of philosophy in revealed theology is necessarily a subordinate one. But reason can demonstrate with certainty the truths of natural theology, as we have already seen. Thus, we are presented with two kinds of theology by St. Thomas, which seem to have little in common except the fact that certain 'preambles of faith' such as the existence of God belong to both.

As we rejected the excessive confidence in reason in St. Thomas' natural theology, we must now reject his conception of revealed theology, because it destroys the independence of reason in relation to dogma and thereby reduces the value of its contribution to theology. His fundamental error here, it seems to me, is to be found in his view of revelation and faith.

Modern Biblical criticism and theology have led to a view of revelation entirely different from that of St. Thomas, and though the modern view is still ruled out by Roman Catholics and Fundamentalists, it is widely accepted by others. While St. Thomas conceives of revelation as an impartation of truths to passive minds which brought nothing from their own experience and reflection to their interpretation of its meaning, modern scholars now think of it as coming through historical events and the response of inspired men to them. The events constitute the 'objective' factor, the 'response' constitutes the 'subjective' factor, in revelation. If we accept this view, we cannot reduce the meaning of revelation to articles of faith or 'dogmas' formulated once and for all by the Church. As the historical events of revelation are concrete and far from simple, their meaning can never be exhausted by dogmas as formulated by any age. Such dogmas are necessary and valuable attempts to define the meaning, but they cannot comprehend the full meaning, of these events.

We must not, therefore, construct revealed or systematic theology upon articles of faith or dogmas as formulated with finality by the Church, but must go behind these to the historical events that gave rise to them. Moreover, we must make use of our own religious experience and reflection in interpreting the meaning of these events. In doing so, of course, we must not suppose that we can dispense with careful study of the interpretations of Christian thinkers of the past whose insight has been illuminating and profound; and we must not cut ourselves off from the collective experience of the Church as a whole. If we do, our interpretations will be the products of nothing but our own limited understanding and personal experience. But nothing can absolve us from the responsibility of trying to understand for ourselves through unrestricted study what the revelation in the Bible really says to us. Though this surrender of final and authoritative statements of the articles of faith may seem a serious loss, there are compensations that more than make up for it. The formulation of the articles of faith in St. Thomas' time was the product of many forces that had played upon the Church for over a thousand years, including ways of thinking, such as that of Neo-Platonism and Aristotelianism, wholly foreign to the spirit of the Bible. The formulations of dogmas accepted by the Protestant churches in later periods are no less fallible. Thus, in rejecting the finality of articles of the faith as formulated at any given time, our minds are freed from errors and preconcep-

tions as to its meaning and we are enabled to study it afresh
with the aid of all the scholarship we can muster.

Corresponding to the change we have noticed in recent thinking about revelation is a change in the conception of faith.
Faith in the revelation recorded in the Bible is not an act of intellectual assent commanded by the will, as in St. Thomas'
view, but a response of the whole self to the Divine Life that has
disclosed itself. This response arises from a vision of the divine
truth manifested in the historical events culminating in Christ,
and as such is not to be regarded as irrational. It is true, of
course, that truth about the infinite cannot be fully comprehended by the finite reason, and that spiritual things cannot but
seem foolishness to sinful men. But faith is not a blind leap
that has to be made by an act of the will under the authority of
the Church; it is based upon an insight, though one that cannot
be demonstrated to be true, into spiritual Reality and Good.

If this conception of revelation and faith is true, reason in
systematic theology should not be restricted to the subordinate
role of clarifying and drawing out the implications of revelation.
Reason must also take the responsibility for interpreting the
meaning of the revelation independently in the light of the best
Biblical scholarship and of religious experience and reflection.
Moreover, nothing can or should prevent reason from analyzing
the evidence that supports faith in the revelation and testing it
by evidence drawn from other sources. In short, reason must be
free, not merely to clarify and elaborate the 'articles of faith'
which are its 'principles,' but also to examine and evaluate them
critically in the light of reason and experience.

2. If St. Thomas' Catholic theory of revealed theology errs in
identifying revelation with the articles of faith of the Church
and in confining the function of philosophy to that of a handmaid of theology, Karl Barth's Neo-Protestant theory errs in
its narrow view of the revelation in the Bible and in its insistence that philosophy shall have no part in systematic theology. His theory, as stated in his *Dogmatik,* may be summarized
as follows: The task of dogmatic theology is to examine the language used by the Church in its proclamation of the Word. The
ability of the theologian to understand the Word with clarity

and certainty depends not upon any rational or other faculty of his own, but upon the possibility given him by the faith that is awakened in him by God. Similarly, his interpretation of the Word must be derived from the Word itself and from no other source. The use of any definite philosophy in interpreting it may distort its meaning by introducing another criterion and content than its own. For the Word judges man, and is not judged by him. The Word is the ultimate norm by which the validity of any theology is to be judged.

The strength of this position, for any Protestant, lies in its emphasis upon the fact that revealed theology must be based primarily upon the revelation of God in the Bible. It is also right in stressing the fact, neglected by many Liberal Protestants, that the revelation in the Bible is normally mediated by the Church and that the proclamation of the Church should be faithful to that revelation. Only in this way can the message of the Church be preserved against contemporary perversions of it, e.g. extreme Modernism, Rationalism, and Humanism, and at the same time be brought to bear upon the need of the time. Finally, Barth is justified in insisting that, to carry out this vital task, the theologian of the Church should let the Bible speak to him directly and not allow other sources of truth to stand in the way of his listening intently to its message. Whatever learning of any sort he may possess must be in the background as he listens to the Word addressed to him.

If Barth had said only this much, all Protestant Christians like myself for whom the Bible is the supreme authority would have had to agree with him. But his reaction against the Rationalism, Naturalism, and Modernism of the last few generations has been dominated by a sharply polemical purpose and spirit. As a result, he has spurned every attempt to come to terms with the modern mind as if it meant an abandonment of the revelation in the Bible. This has led him into two fatal errors.

First, he has narrowed the task of theology in an intolerable way. This is seen most clearly in his attack upon Christian Apologetics. There is no time to go into the nature of Apologetics and its relation to revealed theology in this essay. But there is clearly a need for some, if not all, Christian theologians to work with Christian philosophers in developing Christian Apologetics that will speak to those outside the Church. If the Church is a missionary community and if it must convert the minds of men, the task of Christian Apologetics is indispensable. It may be true that revealed theology and Apologetics should usually be practiced by different theologians, the former by those like Barth who speak mainly to the Church, the other by those like Paul Tillich who have a mission also to those outside the Church. But it is surely part of the task of revealed theology to state the meaning of the Christian revelation in terms that are intelligible to the world and to defend it against alternative world-views and ways of life.

Second, Barth's conception of revealed theology itself is viti-ated by his refusal to use the powers of reason freely in interpret-ing it. This is illustrated most clearly by his insistence that rea-son shall not 'judge' the Word by another criterion external to it, e.g. a philosophical norm of truth or world-view or anthro-pology. As we have seen, this is a valuable warning against read-ing an alien world-view or doctrine of man into the Bible and demands of the theologian that he listen to what the Bible itself says. Barth asserts that the Word is always self-validating: that God is speaking and what He is saying can be known with cer-tainty. Since he distinguishes the Word spoken by God from the words of the Bible, he escapes Biblical literalism or fundamental-ism. But because of this distinction he is tempted into arbitrary and subjective interpretations of the Word. Moreover, he seems to have no doubt about these interpretations.

3. But if both the ecclesiastical dogmatism of St. Thomas and the Biblical dogmatism of Barth are rejected, what conception of revealed or systematic theology is possible? Something at once more creative and more difficult than their dogmatic concep-tions of theology: the attempt freely to think out afresh the meaning of the revelation recorded in the Bible as a whole, with the help of the best Biblical scholarship and theological think-ing of the past and present. The freedom with which the theo-logian approaches this task must, of course, be a responsible free-dom. He speaks not only for himself but as a member of the Christian community. Therefore, he must not cultivate and

proudly display his own idiosyncrasies of experience and interpretation. He must know and respect the work of other Christian thinkers, past and present, even if he cannot accept it at many points. He must also attempt to speak from the center rather than the periphery of the Christian community, defending no partial or sectarian interpretation of its faith but the essence and heart of it.

But the theologian must be free in his thinking. For his primary task is to penetrate to the essence of the Biblical revelation, discover its unity beneath the diversity of its expressions, and distinguish it from the accidental accretions which obscure or distort its real meaning. This is a more difficult task than that of the dogmatic theologian. For it requires not merely the ordering and rationalizing of all the dogmas of the Church or the supposed dogmas of the Bible, but the independent examination of the revelation and the discrimination of its primary from its secondary elements. Hence it demands not so much dialectical skill like that of St. Thomas, or vast theological learning like that of Barth, as religious insight based upon spiritual sensitivity and personal religious experience like that of St. Augustine.

But this is not all. Theology demands an understanding of the needs of men, of what has been called the human predicament, and of the way in which the Christian revelation can meet these needs. In other terms, theology must involve an understanding of the relevance of the faith to the human situation both in general and in contemporary life. This demands a profound insight into the human soul and a knowledge of the social forces that help or hinder spiritual growth. For theology, though it is theoretical in its method, is practical in its aim. It will not do to say, with some contemporary theologians, that theology is wholly practical, for it must make clear the truth about God and His love if it is to show men the way to salvation. On the other hand, the theologian must never forget that the knowledge of God is for the sake of the love and service of God in which lies man's salvation. Therefore, he must not only expound the meaning of the faith but also show how it answers the questions and meets the needs of men.

Systematic theology, as so conceived, is as dangerous as it is difficult. It is safer to stay on the beaten path and confine oneself to the exposition and arrangement of dogmas accepted on the authority of the Church or supposedly found in the Bible. If one thinks independently, one is likely to incur criticism from the custodians of orthodoxy. One is also likely to fall into errors due to his own limited experience, insight, and knowledge. One may, quite unconsciously, put himself at the mercy of the winds of doctrine of his time, winds that blow from every quarter and may be adverse to the Christian faith. Independent thinking in any field is dangerous; in theology it is more dangerous than elsewhere because theology deals with the supreme truth about reality and the ultimate good of man.

In view of these difficulties and dangers of an independent theology, it is to be expected that relatively few Christians in each generation will take upon themselves the burden and the risk of it. Perhaps it is well that this is so. In theology, as in philosophy, few men are genuinely creative, and strong pressure is exerted upon those who teach and write about theology to think along traditional lines. But it is essential to the health of the Church that independent and creative theologians should be at least tolerated. Even if they are regarded by most with suspicion and distrust, their new insights may be gradually assimilated by other theologians and by the Church at large. Since they are fallible, some of their most cherished convictions as well as tentative conjectures will have to be rejected by the Church. Their misplaced emphases and exaggerations will have to be modified lest their partial insights be mistaken for the whole truth. Thus, Origen's belief in the pre-existence of souls was condemned, though he was one of the most creative theologians of the early Church; and St. Augustine's theology of grace, though he was one of the greatest thinkers in the whole history of the Church, has to be qualified because of its one-sidedness and its consequent threat to human freedom and responsibility.

But the dangers of an independent theology must not blind us to the fact that it is essential to the healthy development of Christian thought. Synthetic theologians like St. Thomas and John Calvin would have been impossible without the work of creative theologians like St. Augustine and Martin Luther. It can also be shown, in my opinion, that the greatest of synthetic theologians, St. Thomas, is great in large part because he so often breaks the bonds imposed upon his thinking by his conception of theology and thinks out the meaning and implication of the Christian revelation in the light of his own religious experience, as in his fine treatment of the analogical meaning of the names applied to God. 'The question of the proper language of theology,' as Barth says, 'is ultimately to be answered only with prayer and the life of faith.' [9]

THE USE AND ABUSE OF PHILOSOPHY

It is obvious that, if the account of Revealed Theology we have given is correct, philosophy is more than a handmaid of theology, since reason must interpret independently the meaning of revelation, defend it against its opponents, and show its relevance to human need. It is impossible even to elucidate the faith, much less to defend and apply it, without the help of philosophy. Philosophy is nothing but the attempt to think as clearly, coherently, and comprehensively as possible about the nature of ultimate reality and value. Since revelation has disclosed something important about ultimate reality and value, and since the meaning of its disclosure must be stated by rational beings in general terms, it is inevitable that the general categories and conclusions of philosophy should be used to explain and defend it. If no philosophy exists that is an adequate vehicle of its meaning, it must create a philosophy that is adequate. But a philosophy cannot be created out of nothing. It must be fashioned out of the materials that have been prepared by previous philosophical effort. It was natural, therefore, that for a considerable period of time a new religion like Christianity should be content to adapt to its uses the best philosophy that was at hand.

But there is a danger in the way theologians have often used philosophy, and it is this danger that has led to periodic demands from Tertullian to Barth for a separation of theology from philosophy. Though philosophy as such has no norm or doctrine of its own, philosophy has given rise to particular philosophies that do have norms and doctrines of their own. When the Christian revelation is expressed in the terms of one of these philosophies, the norm and doctrine of the philosophy are likely to be imposed upon it. If that philosophy is taken to be in possession of ultimate truth, its errors are introduced into theology along with its truths. There can be no doubt, it seems to me, that many errors have been incorporated into Christian theology in this way, e.g. those of Neo-Platonism through St. Augustine, those of Aristotle through St. Thomas, those of Spinoza and the Romanticists through Schleiermacher, and those of Hegel through many nineteenth-century Christian thinkers. The only defense against this danger is for the theologian to modify or abandon the philosophy he is using wherever he sees it to be inconsistent with his Christian faith. But he will often fail to detect inconsistencies that do not lie on the surface, especially when they spring from the half-hidden assumptions of the philosophy he is using. His failure will be the greater in proportion as he abandons his critical attitude toward that philosophy and assumes that it is authoritative. He is, of course, more likely to do this if he is not primarily a constructive thinker in philosophy but a theologian eager to find a complete and dependable framework for the interpretation of his faith.

It is not to be wondered at, therefore, that St. Augustine accepted and made full use of the Neo-Platonic philosophy which had helped to convince him of the spiritual nature of reality. But the Neo-Platonic dualism of time and eternity, the theory of evil as privation, and other doctrines played havoc with his thinking as a Christian at certain points. Because he was a constructive thinker in philosophy, however, he was able again and again to break through the categories and refute the conclusions of Neo-Platonic philosophy, especially where his own personal experience and the historical crisis of his time made manifest to him what was new in the Christian revelation. In the case of St. Thomas, there is an even greater dependence upon, though by no means a slavish adherence to, the philosophy of Aristotle, who is quoted again and again as *the* authority in philosophy. Where there is an obvious inconsistency between Aristotle and the Christian faith, e.g. on the Creation of the world or the immortality of the individual soul, St. Thomas abandons 'the philosopher.' At other points, he modifies or supplements Aristotle's doctrine to make room for an article of faith, e.g. in his addition of the 'infused' Christian virtues to the 'acquired' virtues of Aristotle's Ethics. But there are many points where he was not independent enough, e.g. in his treatment of God's knowledge and will where the influence of Aristotle's doctrine of the self-contemplation and self-sufficiency of the Prime Mover is painfully evident. It is important to note, however, that many modern Protestants have freed themselves from the dangerous compromises of medieval theologians with Greek philosophy, only to fall into fatal compromises with Hegelian Idealism or Evolutionary Naturalism.

The conclusion we should draw from all of this, it seems to me, is that natural and revealed theology must use philosophy but must recognize the inadequacy of every philosophy to express fully the Christian faith. Therefore, it must be critical and circumspect in its use of any particular philosophy. To achieve this critical attitude, it must be more rather than less philosophical itself, since only long experience with philosophy makes one fully aware of the limitations as well as the strength of every philosophy.

This should not, however, encourage a feeling of complacency in theologians about theology. Theology, like philosophy, is a product of the finite and fallible reason of man. Its understanding of the Christian revelation is never complete, as we saw, and its expression in rational terms of what it does understand is never perfect. Moreover, theology, like philosophy, is the work of men whose reason has been obscured and distorted by sin. It is amusing—and yet tragic—to read denunciations by theologians of philosophy as the work of proud, rebellious reason, and then to witness them display their own pride in defending their positions and their lack of charity in attacking their opponents.

The truth is, the task of theology and philosophy alike will always remain unfinished, because we are finite creatures. Yet we are unwilling to admit it even to ourselves lest the insecurity that is our lot should show itself. What we must recognize is that, however seriously we should take the task of theology, we can never find our security in any theology, but only in faith. As St. Augustine saw, we must live our lives in faith and the hope that springs from it. Though our efforts to understand may bring glimpses of truth now and then, full vision cannot come to us in this life. There is food for thought—and charity— in this.

NOTES

1. St. Thomas recognizes this, of course, and later in the *Summa Theologica* discusses the 'personal' attributes of God, such as love, justice, and mercy, which are derived from the Christian revelation.
2. Op. cit. ch. IV.
3. Op. cit. ch. XI.
4. Nature, Man and God, Lectures V-X.
5. Ibid. Lecture I.
6. Ibid. Lecture XX.
7. Temple, William, op. cit. p 519.
8. *Summa Theologica*, 1.
9. Barth, Karl, *Credo*, p. 186.

The Language of Theology

BY WILBUR MARSHALL URBAN

○

I

In his book, *The Incarnate Lord,* the Anglican theologian, L. S. Thornton, writes of the language of theology as follows. 'The language of religion in its beginnings is poetic, symbolic and pictorial. It registers primitive reactions to experience in crude mythological images. With the stage of reflective thought more general concepts appear, constructed from wider generalizations of experience, individual, social and historical, moral and rational. Yet these wider concepts for the most part *retain traces of earlier mythological forms and imagery* [italics mine]. A third stage is reached in which scientific observation and rational reflection develop an abstract terminology of their own which has a different genealogical descent from that of religious terminology proper.'

No one would, I suppose, question the truth of this account of the first two stages. Certainly I should not, for elsewhere I have myself written of the language of religion and find it of the same general character. It is rather with the account of the third stage of the development of theological language, the so-called 'abstract terminology,' that I should take issue. For on this point depends, I believe, not only a right understanding of the lan-

NOTE: The material in this chapter is taken from Mr. Urban's *Humanity and Deity,* published by George Allen and Unwin, Ltd., London, who have kindly given permission to include it in the present volume.

57

guage of theology, but ultimately in large part the meaning of that language and the truth of what it says.

The terminology of this third stage, according to Father Thornton, has a different genealogical descent from that of religious terminology proper. This is in part true, but only in part. Christian theology was indeed possible only by the translation of the language of religion, the Heavenly Father of prayer and praise, into the metaphysical idiom of Greek philosophy, but this idiom was itself, in large part, of religious origin. It was for this reason that Christian thinkers could use it and that it was possible for men to say that Plato was the Greek Moses and that, pagan though he was, he touched the very gates of heaven.

This, then, is the theme of this paper—that the language of Christian theology is a translation of the language of religion, with all its poetic and dramatic character, into terms of greater generality—into, as it were, another idiom—but that this translation takes place without loss of meaning, without loss of the *vis poetica*, without which there is no religious expression, and, therefore, without loss of the *vis religiosa*. That, to express it differently, the Heavenly Father of prayer and praise and the *Ens Perfectissimum* of Christian theology are one and the same. Before developing my theme, however, let me say a word on the general question of the relation of language to knowledge and truth.

The ancient dictum that there is no thought without language is, I believe, essentially and profoundly true. Any denial of it rests, I think it can be shown, upon misunderstandings and equivocations. But the truth of this dictum implies a further truth, namely that it is only in language appropriate to the object of our thought that any significant discourse can be carried on. Theology is discourse about God. Meaningful statements about Him are possible only in a language appropriate to the universe of discourse in which our converse takes place. God may, indeed, be a mathematician—for His perfections are infinite—but it is certain that men cannot talk about Him meaningfully in mathematical terms. If they should try to do so, they would be talking nonsense, as indeed they often do when they try to apply mathematics to the notion of the Trinity. As Aristotle rightly saw, it is a mark of intelligence to understand to what things mathematics can and cannot be applied, but this is but one aspect of a more general and fundamental philosophical truth—namely that the only way of determining reality at all is in those forms or categories in terms of which meaningful statements about it are possible. Since, however, statements are always linguistic expressions, the problem of the relation of language to reality is the basal problem of all knowledge. It is a still greater mark of intelligence to understand this more ultimate truth.

The language of religion is then, as Father Thornton tells us, poetic, symbolic, and pictorial. Its primary forms are the lyrical and the dramatic. It is impossible to express the religious consciousness directly except in the modes of prayer and praise. He who can neither pray nor sing is not only religiously inarticulate, but finds himself inhibited at the very sources of religious experience itself. There is, however, a more indirect form, the dramatic, which has its source in the language of myth. The primary religious experiences, as Father Thornton also rightly tells us, are 'registered in mythical images,' but such images are by no means so crude as he supposes, for 'behind the myth,' as Berdyaev puts it so excellently, 'are concealed the greatest realities, the original phenomena of the spiritual life.'

It is of the utmost importance that there be no misunderstanding here. Religion is not myth—even 'permanent myth,' as Reinhold Niebuhr would say. Religion merely makes use of the language of the myth as the indispensable material for the symbolic expression of the historical element in religion. To say with Paul Tillich, that 'Christian history is irreparably ruined, but Christian myth remains the most compelling expression of man's timeless spiritual experience evolved in any religion,' is to my mind fatally to misrepresent the situation. Christian myth does not have to be 'completely severed from history,' as he further says, 'in order to convey its full freight of metaphysical truth,' for the very good reason that the two have never been thus identified. In so far as theology is concerned, its very existence depends upon the possibility of the translation of the dramatic language of religion into an idiom in which precisely this full freight of metaphysical truth, without which religion is nothing, can be adequately expressed.

With this conception of the language of religion it is now possible to understand the language of theology. The dogmas of theology, writes William James, 'are secondary products, like translations of a text into another tongue.' In this, as we have seen, he is in principle right, but everything depends, as we have also seen, upon a right understanding of the tongue into which the intuitions of faith are translated. If, following a popular view of so-called liberal religion, he supposes, as he seems to do, that the tongue into which the translation takes place is one alien to religion itself, and that religion without dogma would be the ideal, he is surely wrong, as it is one of the objects of this paper to show.

Here again, it is important that there should be no misunderstanding. This insistence upon the virtual identity of the language of religion with the language of theology does not mean, as some would say, that theology is 'myth rationalized.' It merely means that the language of theology, however abstract it may become, never loses its kinship with the dramatic language of religion. Nor does it mean that theology is merely a 'dialectic of symbols,' as Recéjac and other extreme mystics have thought. It means merely that we must recognize the partly symbolic character of the language of theology and realize the fundamental role of 'symbolism as a theological principle.'

This derivation of the language of theology from that of religion would, I suppose, delight the so-called logical positivist into whose hands, it may be thought, I have unwittingly played. The language of religion is emotive and, therefore, since the language of theology is a translation of the former, it is emotive also. All utterances about God and His nature are, therefore, in their extraordinary vocabulary, non-sensical, since they refer to nothing—any talk about God, whether religious or theological, being *blab blab,* to use the elegant terms of one of the more irresponsible representatives of the position. It seems hardly necessary in this presence to consider seriously a position so obviously impossible to maintain, and one, moreover, which in responsible philosophical circles is equally obviously on the wane. I should, however, like to make one comment in this connection, for it is not without significance for the further development of my thesis.

The language of theology, like the language of religion from which it is derived, has its emotive aspect. But it does not at all follow that for this reason it has no reference. No expression, even the most emotive, is, as I have shown elsewhere, wholly without a referend; the task is to find out what the referend really is. There is another ancient dictum which is also essentially and profoundly true, namely that we cannot talk about that which is not. We may, of course, be mistaken as to the object of our discourse. We may also be mistaken as to the mode of existence of the object—even in physical science men sometimes suppose that a thing exists, in the sense of being sensuously observable, when it does not. But all this does not alter the fact that, whatever be the universe of discourse, when men can communicate with one another, and when the one can understand what the other says, that about which they talk exists. This also, I believe to be one of the most fundamental of all philosophic truths.

Theology, or theological thinking, may take either of two approaches: thinking about God, and thinking from man and nature to God. These correspond to two well-recognized divisions, namely dogmatic and natural or rational theology. Thinking about God, His nature and His acts, takes place within a universe of discourse already determined by the presupposition of His existence and belief in Him. This belief may be conceived as established solely by revelation or solely by reason, or by both, but the prior determination is already assumed. Thinking to God, on the other hand, always proceeds from man and nature, either logically from some *a priori* intuition, or, empirically, from the things that are seen to the things that are unseen. One of the main problems of philosophical theology has always revolved about the relation of the two.

In the earlier centuries of Christian thought the two were not clearly distinguished. Neither St. Augustine nor St. Anselm found it necessary to make the sharp division which later reflection

seemed to demand, and Anselm at least was often chided for his
'neglect.' It was only later that the distinction became, so to
speak, the working theory of Christian theology and philosophy.
The doctrine that 'the truth of the intelligible things of God is
twofold, one to which the inquiry of reason can attain the other
which surpasses the whole range of human reason,' a doctrine
enunciated by St. Thomas in a number of places, became the
authoritative position of classical theology. Christian theology
has come to insist upon this difference, but it also maintains and
has always maintained, that the two are intimately related. On
this point we shall have something to say in the sequel. As illustrations of the two theologies we may take the *Cur Deus Homo*
and the *Proslogium* of St. Anselm. In the first, faith inquires of
the intellect why God became man; in the second it inquires of
that same intellect whether there is any God to become man. Let
us begin with the answer to the first question, and by an analysis
of the argument seek to understand its character and its form.

II

The object of the *Cur Deus Homo* is the search for the reasons
of the Incarnation. That God did become man is, for Anselm, a
fact of the religious order—a dogma accepted on faith. The problem is to understand the fact. It is, as he says, *fides quaerens intellectum*, and it is the reason alone that can give understanding
in the sense that he desires.

The Incarnation, according to Anselm, follows necessarily
from the need of redemption. Sin is an offense against the maj-
esty of God. In spite of His goodness, God cannot pardon sin
without compounding with honor and justice. On the other
hand, he cannot revenge Himself on man for His offended honor,
for sin is an offense of infinite degree and therefore demands infinite satisfaction; which means that He must either destroy humanity or inflict upon it the eternal punishments of hell. Now
in either case the goal of creation, the happiness of His creatures,
would be missed and the honor of the Creator compromised.
There is but one way for God to escape this dilemma without
affecting His honor, and that is to arrange for some kind of sat-

isfaction. He must have infinite satisfaction because the offense is immeasurable. Now in so far as man is a finite being, and incapable of satisfying divine justice in an infinite measure, the infinite Being Himself must take the matter in hand; He must have recourse to substitution. Hence the necessity of the Incarnation. God becomes man in Christ; Christ suffers and dies in our stead; thus He acquires infinite merit and the right to an equivalent recompense. But since the world belongs to the Creator and nothing can be added to its treasures, the recompense that by right belongs to Christ falls to the lot of the human race in which He is incorporated: humanity is pardoned, forgiven, and saved.

I am well aware, of course, that this way of talking and thinking is sufficiently remote from our present intellectual climate and has been largely repudiated by what is called liberal theology. It is said to be too legalistic and to bear the stamp of the spirit of chivalry and of the feudal customs that inspired and conditioned it. With this aspect of Anselm's argument I am, however, not concerned, although I personally believe that it contains an abiding element of truth which will survive our temporary sentimentalism and the attempts of liberalism to naturalize the supernatural. What I am concerned with is the more general question of the type of argument involved and the kind of 'reasons' it embodies. For any theory of the Atonement—any attempt to answer such a question as 'Why God became man?'—would, I think, involve language and reasoning of this general type. It may be thought that we should not ask such questions —or indeed talk at all about such an object as the God-man; but if we do we must think and talk more or less as did Anselm. In this universe of discourse only such language is appropriate and reasons can be only of this general type.

The language in which St. Anselm speaks is human and the reasons he gives apparently anthropomorphic, conditioned not only by the way in which men think, but also, to an extent, by the way in which men of his time thought and spoke. He speaks of God's goodness, of His honor, and His justice. These moral predicates when applied to the Divine are, however, even for Anselm, and still more for later classical theology, although related to the human, not man's but God's. Granted that there is a God and that He is identical with absolute or Sovereign Goodness (and this postulate is the basis of all theology), then the Incarnation follows. Between these attributes—honor, justice, and equity—when attributed to God in an absolute sense, there subsist relations of such a character that a revelation of God in man necessarily follows. The reasons are value reasons or, in more technical terms, axiological. This is, however, the character of all ultimate reasons, for as Whitehead rightly says, all ultimate reasons involve aim at value. The fact that the necessity in the argument is moral or axiological does not, however, exclude the fact that it is rational and logical also. The sheer logic of Anselm's *Cur Deus Homo* is as much a part of it as is the logic of the *Proslogium*. The relation of the logical to the axiological is a fundamental problem of theology as it is of philosophy, but that is another story.

Illustrations of this way of thinking could be taken from all forms of religion which have developed far enough to have a theology. It is, however, with Christian theology that we are primarily concerned, and it is to this that we shall confine our thought.

Why did God become man? Why, it is asked also, did He create the world of creatures with all its manifold variety and an apparent purposelessness? And it is interesting to see how men answered. The reason given is the principle of perfection or completeness, the principle of the Good, with which Deity is identified. But we may also ask, Why did God, the very essence of perfection and completeness (including His own self-sufficiency), create at all? It is enlightening to see how St. Thomas answered that question. God must create, he holds—not, to be sure, by any external compulsion, but by an inner axiological necessity which springs out of His very nature as the principle of the Good.

Speaking of the love of God, St. Thomas writes: 'Love, which works good to all things, pre-existing overflowingly in the Good, moved itself to creation as befits the superabundance by which all things are generated. . . The Good by being extends its goodness to all things. For as our sun, not by choosing or taking thought, but by merely being, enlightens all things, so the Good . . . by its mere existence sends forth upon all things the beams of its Goodness.' [1]

Of this passage it has been said that in it 'the phraseology of the primitive Christian conception of a loving Father in Heaven has been translated into the Platonic Idiom.' This is doubtless true, as we have already indicated and shall see more fully presently. The issue for theology, however, is whether in this translation the primitive language has lost the *vis religiosa*. That it has not is our essential thesis. So far as this particular passage is concerned, once the identification of God with the Sovereign Good is made—an identification that is the necessary postulate of theology—the Creation no less than the Incarnation necessarily follows. It is indeed the intrinsic nature of the Good to extend its Goodness to all things.

This way of thinking, and the translation it involves, are, I think, implicit not only in classical theology but in traditional European philosophy also, from which theology was never completely separated and for which the primacy of the Good or value has always been a cardinal principle. But it continued to be the natural idiom of the entire rationalistic movement of the seventeenth and eighteenth centuries. From this movement I shall choose only one figure, but that an important one—namely Leibniz, who, as is well known, was as much at home in theological as in mathematical reasoning, and to whom it was natural not only to name the name of God, but to use that concept in his most abstract and metaphysical reasoning.

I should add greatly to the force of my argument and to the significance of this paper if I could develop this point at some length, but time will not permit. It must suffice to point out that Leibniz employs the same language and the same axiological reasoning as does Anselm and St. Thomas, using the Goodness of God, or the 'principle of perfection' as he also calls it, in his metaphysical reasoning and in his rational or natural theology. The work of Leibniz in which this way of thinking is most in evidence is his famous *Theodicy,* which has as its main topics the Goodness of God, the liberty of man, and the origin of evil, but it is determinative in all his works, especially in the *Principles of Nature and of Grace*. Of the former work it has been said that 'Leibniz was merely continuing the tradition of Platonic rationalism in Christian theology,' and this is true, for his chief topic is the Goodness of God and what necessarily and logically follows from it. This rationalistic tradition in Christian theology is, however, as it is now beginning to appear, the condition of there being any theology whatsoever.

In the preceding pages we have become familiar with a type of thinking that is not only natural to the religious consciousness, but, as I also think, inevitable if the mind is to think religiously at all—that is about God, His nature, and His acts. The principle upon which this thinking proceeds, the 'principle of perfection,' as Leibniz calls it, was predetermined by the Greek philosophical tradition. The identification of God with the Good in Christian theology was made possible by the assumption, either explicit or implicit, of the ultimate inseparability of the Good or Value and Being. This is the major premise of all Christian as of all Greek thinking.

The primary source of this identification of God with the Good is, of course, Plato in the *Republic* and the *Timaeus*. If we are to assume that the idea of the Good in the *Republic*, the ground and source of all being, and the Creator who figures in the *Timaeus* are one and the same, then the idea of the Absolute Good is identical with the idea of God. Interpreters of Plato, both ancient and modern, have disputed endlessly over this question, and into this dispute I have no intention of entering here. It is enough for our purpose that this identity was assumed by Christian theology and constituted its basis.

There can be no question, I think, that this is so. 'If the idea of God is taken as standing for what the Schoolmen called the *ens perfectissimum*, the summit of the hierarchy of being, the only satisfying object of contemplation and adoration, there can be little doubt that the idea of the Good was the God of Plato and there can be none at all that it became also the God of Aristotle and one of the elements or aspects of the God of the theologians and philosophers of the Middle Ages and of nearly all the modern Platonizing poets and philosophers.' This then is undoubtedly the source of the language of Christian theology and, as I have been contending, the language of religion is translatable into it without loss of meaning—in other words, the God of religion and of religious devotion and the God of theology and philosophy are the same. This is the postulate I wish to defend, for it constitutes the initial premise of all theological thinking, and upon the truth of the postulate depends, I believe, the possibility of all theology either dogmatic or rational.

The denial of this postulate has been the essential point of all critics of classical theology from Lactantius to the present time. As Tolstoy puts it in his famous *Critique of Dogmatic Theology*, these theologians 'are not talking about God but about something else.' And, with his customary forthrightness, he tells them 'to go to their father the Devil, the father of all lies.' It is this continuous opposition between the *Deus vivus* of religion and the *deus philosophorum*, the ancient battle of Lactantius against the God of the philosophers, the battle of Duns Scotus for the 'God of Willing' as opposed to the 'God of Being,' of Luther for the living God of scripture against the God of the scholastics, of Kierkegaard and his congeners against all dialectical theology.

The latest philosopher to take up this issue is A. O. Lovejoy in his book, *The Great Chain of Being*, one of the more important of modern works in philosophy. He, too, insists that the God of religion is not the God of theologians and philosophers, or, as he puts it, they are not one God but two. For him Christian thought contains an irreconcilable contradiction, and upon this contradiction the entire structure of classical theology, both dogmatic and rational, suffers shipwreck. Since he presents his thesis with all the logical technique of the sophisticated modern philosopher, it will be well for us to follow his argument at this point.

What classical theology did, so he holds, was 'to convert by a bold logical inversion the Good as the *ens perfectissimum* into the God of creation into a self-transcending Fecundity. As it was phrased in the Middle Ages, *omne bonum est diffusivum sui*. This inversion seemed to them possible without the notion of Self-sufficing Perfection losing its original implications upon which all theological thinking depends.' It seemed possible also to do this without the notion of God losing the *vis religiosa*, the dramatic or, if you will, anthropomorphic character which alone makes it the object of religious devotion. This conversion, Lovejoy holds, as have many, is impossible, and as a result there has been from the beginning, at the very heart of Christian theology, a contradiction of both practical and theoretical import, one that destroys Christianity not only as a way of thought but as a way of life also.

This irreconcilable conflict is stated thus. 'God was the idea of the Good, but he was also the idea of Goodness; and although the second attribute was nominally deduced dialectically from the first, no two notions could be more antithetic. The one was the apotheosis of unity, self-sufficiency and quietude, the other of diversity, self transcendence and fecundity. The one God was the goal of the "way up," of that ascending process by which the finite soul, turning from all created things, took its way back to the immutable Perfection in which alone it could rest. The other God was the source and informing energy of that descending process by which being flows through all the levels of possibility down to the lowest.' In simpler terms, those two notions of the Good or value, in our modern terms, are, he holds, in absolute contradiction.

Theoretically, we are told, this contradiction did not greatly trouble the medieval mind, for which the notion of the coincidence of opposites (*coincidentia oppositorum*) in the Absolute was an accepted principle. But—and this is the significant thing in his contention—this discrepancy was not merely between two abstract ideas, but also between two practical attitudes. This conflict in the notion of the Good involved a fundamental conflict in men's notion of the Christian way of life, for 'the doctrine of the divine attributes, and far more significantly, a theory of ultimate value, was at the same time the definition of the objective of human life. The final good of almost all Western philosophers and theologians for a millennium consisted in some approximation to the Divine nature, whether that mode was defined as imitation or contemplation or absorption. The Absolute Being, utterly unlike any creature in nature, was yet the *primum exemplar omnium.* The God in whom man was to find his own fulfillment was then not one God but two.'

This, then, is the issue, both theoretical and practical. It is, of course, ultimately theoretical, as all fundamental issues are; but let us begin with the practical aspect. Now it seems to me that nothing is clearer than that the entire story of Christian life and piety constitutes a refutation of this position and manifests a continual reconciliation of these two opposites. I do not mean that every individual believer has been able to reconcile completely contemplation of the Perfect Being with devotion to the God of Goodness and the expression of this devotion in works of mercy and of love. But the great saints and mystics have, and it is precisely this which constitutes their outstanding significance for the philosophical theologian. The fact that the two attitudes are not contradictory in life creates the presumption that they are reconcilable in theory also. It is this, I believe and shall attempt to show, philosophical theology has been able to do. If this can be shown, I shall have been able to make good my chief thesis with regard to the language of theology.

Here, however, I am afraid I shall have to be a little more technical than I like to be in a paper of this kind. There are two points that I shall try to make. The first concerns the nature of the philosophical notion of the Good with which the notion of God is equated; the second concerns the Thomistic doctrine of analogy in terms of which the doctrine of the Divine predicates was formulated.

Everything turns, in the first place, upon the question of the Platonic and Aristotelian notions of the Good, with which, both for the Greek philosopher and the Christian theologian, the religious notion of God was identified. The assumption that underlies the charge of an irreconcilable contradiction between the two ideas of value—the idea of the Good and the idea of Goodness—is that the Good is an essence in the same sense as the other Platonic essences, such, for instance, as geometrical ideas, the nature of which is merely to be. This assumption is, I believe, quite false. I do not believe that Plato himself, even in the *Republic,* identified the Good with this conception of essence. The famous passage in which the objects of knowledge are said to derive from the Good the gift of being known, and which ascribes to the Good not only 'dignity' but 'power,' seems to belie such a notion. Still less is it the notion of the Good of Aristotle, who ascribes to it the power of final causation. With the question of interpretation, however, I am not chiefly concerned. Even if Plato did identify the Sovereign Good with the other essences, which he did not, he would most certainly be wrong. An adequate phenomenological analysis of value has shown, I think, that it is *toto genere* different from the other essences and that it is precisely this 'power,' of which both Plato and Aristotle speak, which is its essential character. It is indeed of the nature of the Good to extend its goodness to all things.

The conversion of the Good as the *ens perfectissimum* into the God of creation, or as it was phrased *omne bonum est diffusivum sui,* is, I should hold, wholly justified if the nature of the Good or value is properly understood. But this is only the first stage in our argument. The second part consists in showing that this identification of the religious idea of God with the philosophical idea of the Sovereign Good made possible the doctrine of analogy —and with it the conception of the Divine attributes which constitutes the very heart of Christian theology. Here, too, I shall have to be somewhat more technical than I should wish.

From the very beginning of Christian thought the great and continuous problem has been to retain the language of religion and at the same time avoid the anthropomorphism apparently inherent in a literal interpretation of this language. A central problem of theology, from St. Augustine on, has been just this question of the nature of its language. Abelard, in his remarkable *Dialogue between a Philosopher, a Jew and a Christian,* asserts that 'what is said of God in bodily form is not to be understood, as the laity commonly do, corporeally and literally, but allegorically and mystically.' And St. Thomas condemns the extravagances of the anthropomorphite heretics who depicted God with human features. Such anthropomorphism, however, as classical theology, including St. Thomas himself, well understood applied not only to our images but to our speech, not only to the way we envisage the Divine but also to the way in which we talk about Divine things. It was this situation which the doctrine of analogy sought to meet, for it was in its essence a theory of the relation of the language of religion to that of theology and philosophy.

The language of the *Cur Deus Homo* is, as we have seen, apparently anthropomorphic. The predicates applied to the Divine, those of Goodness, honor, justice, et cetera, are, in the first instance, human and conditioned by the way in which they appear in us creatures. We appear to talk of God as though He were a man. Actually, however, even in St. Anselm, that is not the case. But how it is possible for us to use such language about God, and yet not talk about Him as though He were a man, was first made clear by St. Thomas.

The reason this is possible is that we can apply our human qualities analogically to God, in an eminent or absolute degree, and the ground for this possibility is found in an 'analogy of being' between the Creator and the creature. As the result of this relation, the being of the creature is sufficiently analogous (not identical) with that of the Creator to enable us to apply such predicates unequivocally to the Divine. The doctrine of analogy of being rests, in turn, upon the theistic argument and if this argument is denied, there is, as the extreme revelationists insist, no way from man to God.

The details of this doctrine of analogy are of great importance, but I cannot go into them here. I shall content myself with one comment of special moment in the present context.

It is generally recognized that this doctrine is the heart of the classical tradition in Christian theology. Men speak of it as the way in which this theology solved the dilemma of anthropomorphism and agnosticism and this is true, but I wish to consider it and evaluate it from another angle. It is, as I have suggested, the classical solution of the problem of the language of theology. For it shows us how indeed the language of religion and the language of theology are one. We may indeed apply to God the predicates of goodness, justice, love, mercy as we men understand them; otherwise there would be no language of prayer and praise. But we can do so because these predicates, as they are conditioned by the way in which they appear in us creatures, are so related to the same predicates as they appear

eminently in the Divine being that the God of religion, the
Heavenly Father of prayer and praise, and the God of theology
are indeed not two Gods but one and the same.

All this may seem to be unduly technical and sufficiently remote from our main topic and from the interests of this body.
As a matter of fact it goes to the very heart of the matter. The
issue, as we have already seen, far from being a merely technical
matter, important as that aspect of the question is, goes to the
heart of Christian life and faith. It is accordingly from the
practical point of view that the foundations of theology are increasingly attacked. The champion of simple piety also becomes
the enemy of theology. In the name of what he calls vital religion, he, too, often tells us that the God of prayer and praise
and the God of theology are not one God but two.

Of the two forms of attack, that of piety is, if anything, more
inimical to true religion. The skeptical philosopher may be met
in the lists of reason and may, conceivably at least, be overcome
in the battle of dialectic; the champion of piety, on the other
hand, cannot be met at all, for there is no common ground. One
finds this attack where one least expects it. It is something of a
shock to hear an Anglican dean, W. R. Matthews, in his *God
in Christian Thought and Experience,* assert that 'the Deus
philosophicus is not the God and Father of our Lord Jesus
Christ' and that 'we cannot believe in the Deity who emerges
from their [the schoolmen's] logic, not because He is too high,
but because He does not in reality sustain the Christian values.'
On the contrary, so I believe, only such a Deity can really sustain these values.

This leads me to speak briefly of a movement in modern religious thought which, I suppose, is partly the inspiration of the
foregoing attack on the schoolmen's Deity, namely that stemming from Kierkegaard and his congeners.

When, we are told, we forsake the language of religion, the
modes of prayer and praise, our life and thought cease to be
integral and thought breaks up into dialectics. Theology, as
Kierkegaard and his congeners tell us, can never be anything
else than dialectical. Theological thought, being thus dialectical,

is refracted by logic into contradictions and antinomies. Involving as it does the application of our human language and categories to the Divine, it is necessarily antinomical and destructive of religion. Not only does theology break up the original experiences into contradictions but generates those paradoxes of reason, as Kierkegaard calls them, which, being insoluble, serve but to reveal the abyss of alogical meaning which is for him the ground and source of all religious experience.

This is not the place to discuss this, perhaps most fundamental, issue in present-day thought on religion. If nothing else, time would forbid it. But I should like to suggest how closely it is tied up with our present problem.

This movement is really but a very modern and sophisticated form of setting the *Deus vivus* over against the *Deus philosophorum,* the God of the scriptures over against the God of the scholastics—of the God of revelation against the God of reason. But here again the question of language rears its frightful head. Since all statements of revealed religion are expressed, and must be expressed, in language drawn from the world of finite things, they must be interpreted. No doctrine of revelation, however absolute, presupposes that the statements are perfectly literal. God is not man, and human language requires to be read with certain qualifications before it applies to Him. Such qualifications can be justified, however, only on some theory of the relation of the Word of God and the word of man, and this is ultimately possible only upon some rational theory of the relation of the human to the Divine, such as that of St. Thomas. The question of the relation of God to man is logically prior to the question of the truth of any particular revelation.

I am not without a certain sympathy for the extreme revelationist, and for the crisis in religion which has made him possible, but I do not believe that the difficulties in such a position can be stated too strongly. For even if it were true, as he tells us, that God and man stand over against one another as Absolute and relative, Unconditioned and conditioned, and that consequently religion cannot be grounded on anything human but only on God—even if, as is sometimes paradoxically maintained, all that God has to say to man is contrary to human nature and

human reason, must we not still ask, how it is possible that man
should understand at all what God says? The nemesis of extreme
revelationism is sure and certain. If we conceive revelation as a
bolt from the blue and refuse to relate it to the primary intuitions and values of men, as embodied in their language, do we
not end by making revelation itself, and the processes by which
it is received, wholly unintelligible? We insist upon the unique-
ness of our own revelation, but by refusing to relate it to the
element of revelation in the faiths of others, we make it impossible for us both to understand those faiths and to communicate
the essence of our own. In sum, any tenable doctrine of revelation presupposes an understanding of the relation of the Word
of God to the word of man, and this in turn presupposes a relation of the human to the Divine which, in the last analysis, can
be determined only by reason. This brings us to a brief consideration of so-called rational theology in its relation to dogmatic.

III

The theme of this paper is, in terms of critical philosophy,
How is dogmatic theology possible? It is possible, we may say,
if religion itself is possible—that the language of theology is as
meaningful and valid as the language of religion of which it is
the translation and explication. But is religion itself possible?
Is the existence of God—the God about whom both theology
and religion itself speak—credible? The question, how is dogmatic theology possible, is bound up, I believe, with the further
question, how is rational theology possible? Obviously time will
not permit me to go into this question at any length, but the
development of the thesis of this paper would be fatally incomplete without some comment on this point.

The title of the section on rational theology in Kant's *Critique
of the Pure Reason* is 'Critique of all theology.' What Kant saw
clearly is the fact that the two theologies are of one piece, and
that a critique of the one involves a critique of the other also.
In other words, the two theologies hang together, and if they do
not continue to do so, they will, humanly speaking, hang sepa-

rately. It is the way in which they hang together that is the topic of these last paragraphs.

In Father Thornton's account of the language of theology with which in part we took issue, we are told that a third stage is reached (in its development) 'in which scientific observation and rational reflection develop an abstract terminology of their own which has a different genealogical descent from that of religious terminology proper.' This is supposed to apply particularly to that part of theology called natural or rational, which is held to speak an entirely different language—that of science, so to speak, rather than that of religion. This also I should be disposed to deny. As the language of dogmatic theology is integral with that of religion and religious experience, so also is the language of rational theology integral with that of religion and dogma. Christian philosophers were able to develop a Christian theism out of the arguments of Plato and Aristotle because, as they recognized from the beginning, they were talking the same language.

The underlying postulate of all thinking about God, His nature, and His acts is, as we have shown, and as Kant also recognized, the identity of the Idea of God with that of the Sovereign Good, or of the *Ens perfectissimum,* the 'principle of Perfection.' Even revelation, for reasons that we have seen, cannot of itself and alone guarantee this postulate. It is for this reason that Anselm wrote not only the *Cur Deus Homo* but the *Proslogium* also, which, as the title indicates, constituted the prologue to the former. It is thus the necessary prologue, for here faith inquires of the intellect whether God as the *Ens Perfectissimum* is also the *ens realissimum,* that is whether the Good and Being are one and the same.

The reasoning by which Anselm and later Aquinas sought to validate this postulate constitutes the so-called theistic proofs, which not only constituted the center of Christian philosophy but also the heart of the *corpus philosophicum* of the entire European tradition. To make good my thesis at this point I should, of course, have to examine this entire argument; but do not be alarmed, I shall not attempt such an impossible task. Let me merely state in passing that I personally consider the argument

as a whole valid, including even the so-called Platonic or ontological argument. Kant was right, I believe, in holding that the
latter is the presupposition of the other arguments, but wrong in
thinking that it is not valid. I think, moreover, that when he
gave the primacy to the moral or axiological argument he at the
same time gave the clue to the interpretation of the ontological.
So much in passing. Our concern here is wholly with the question of the language of so-called rational theology.

My point then is briefly this, that the language of rational theology is, like that of dogmatic, axiological, and the reasoning
mutatis mutandis of the same general order.

I have been wondering how I could make my point as clearly
and briefly as possible. I think I can perhaps do it best by reference to a comment that Gilson [2] makes upon the Platonic or
Anselmian proof. He makes the point that unless the identity
of the Good and Being is taken as the initial datum, we could
never arrive at the God of religion and theology, but something
else—a merely cosmic principle. The two theologies would be
talking different languages and really not speaking of the same
thing at all. The criticism is frequently made of St. Thomas
that his causal arguments do not suffice to prove the God of religion and that by such argument alone the identification of the
absolute Good and absolute Being cannot be justified. To which
his defenders reply, rightly I believe, that it is only when the
argument is taken as a whole, and with the moral or axiological
argument as its heart, that it becomes an argument for the existence of God, and that actually this is what St. Thomas did.

Be this as it may, the authoritative position of Christian philosophy is, as we have seen, that the truth of the intelligible
things of God is twofold, one to which the inquiry of reason
can attain, the other which surpasses the whole range of human
reason. But while insisting upon this difference, this same Christian thought has also always maintained that the two are intimately and organically related. How then can they be different
and yet thus integrally related the one to the other?

The problem is really much more difficult than appears at
first sight. There is one answer to the question which, while
appearing to be an answer, is really little more than verbal and

formal. Abstractly, we are told, the two theologies are indeed autonomous, but concretely they are not. While in principle there is a certain limited knowledge of God accessible to the human reason alone, actually in practice it is only in the light of revelation that human reason can function adequately and obtain, even within its own limits, a knowledge of God, free from error. Man's natural powers, so we are told, are themselves so weakened by sin that even his natural knowledge of God is clouded and distorted. Grace not only supplies perfections that transcend those possible to nature, but also restores nature to its proper integrity.

But surely this is to give away the entire case for rational theology, and in the end to fall back upon that extreme revelationism which, we have already seen, cannot be maintained. For is it not the entire point of rational theology that the existence and nature of God is known, up to a point at least, by reason alone? And if this is so, must it not be the natural light of reason given to every man who enters into the world—and not a reason that, even if thus 'restored,' has been changed by Grace from its natural character into something else? One can scarcely follow the argument of reason wherever it may lead and at the same time insist upon knowing before hand where it will come out. Anselm, it is true, began the *Proslogium* with a prayer that his intellect should be guided aright, but he had no doubt that what his reason showed to be true would commend itself to the natural reason whether restored by Grace or not.

No, we must, I think, give a quite different answer to this question. The reason why the rational theology of an Aristotle and an Aquinas are, although different, at bottom the same, is that the human reason to which the knowledge of God is accessible is in both cases the natural light of reason given to every one by God at creation. With creation not only is given the *imago Dei* but, since the source of that light is the Eternal Logos, with it also is given a language which is the same for all men and in which the intelligible things of God may be expressed. We must, I think, hold fast to the relative independence of rational theology, but this does not involve any denial of the fundamental organic relation between the two.

This classical Christian philosophy has, I believe, always realized. If Plato and Aristotle spoke a wholly different idiom from the Christian, their God would not be the God of the Christian. On the other hand, if Plato and Aristotle, to say nothing of thinkers more widely remote from us, could not achieve a reasonable belief in God, independently of the images and symbols of a particular revelation, then it would be impossible to show that the God whom these others 'ignorantly worship' is one with the God whom the Christian seeks to declare.

This the founder of the Christian religion Himself fully understood and it is a pity that so many of His followers lack this understanding. Jesus made His appeal in the words, 'Ye believe in God, believe also in me' and not in the form, Ye believe in me, believe also in God. The latter is doubtless for many minds the psychological order, but it is certainly not the logical order. It is only when we come to believe, through our reason, in God as the Sovereign and Eternal Good, and as the ground and goal of our human existence, that we can believe in His own concrete revelation of that Good. It is only if we know that God is, and what He is, that we can acknowledge any revelation as divine. The historical pronouncements of revealed religion presuppose the cosmological pronouncements of religion and the latter the ontological. The *Cur Deus Homo* presupposes the *Proslogium,* as St. Anselm fully saw.

NOTES

1. This passage is found in *De div nom.* IV. 10.
2. *The Spirit of Medieval Philosophy,* p. 60. The entire chapter in which this conception is developed is worthy of careful study.

Theology as Theoretical and Practical Knowledge

BY LEWIS M. HAMMOND

The broad topic suggested by the Executive Committee for this discussion leaves a wide range of liberty of choice of subject matter and mode of treatment; on the other hand, broad liberties entail a correspondingly wide responsibility on the part of the writer to make the proper choices himself. The responsibility in this case, as I understand it, is to present a general introductory discussion of theology first, as a body of knowledge available to mankind and in which human reason plays a part, though a limited one; and second, to consider theology in its practical relation to the Christian life and to human affairs generally. The purpose will be to open up the general field for the more specific discussions to follow.

The validity and usefulness of theology is challenged from two sides nowadays, as it has been during past centuries also. On the one hand, since the object of this science lies beyond the possibility of direct human observation and rational comprehension, its validity has been denied by materialists, positivists, and naturalistic humanists of every century, whether they were natural scientists, social scientists, or philosophers. On the other hand, there has always been a tradition of deeply religious and pious people who also reject theology as inimical to true religion, as dangerous to the faith, and as the handiwork of the devil.

Both types of objections reflect the same basic difficulties that

79

are inherent in the unique claims and the unique position of the science of theology—using the term science here in its radical meaning of *scientia*, knowledge in a broader sense than experimental knowledge. For example, theology must attempt to give a rational discussion of a kind of knowledge that transcends reason; to treat of the supernatural by employing discourse proportionate to the cognitive powers of human nature; to attempt to describe and justify a kind of knowledge that is based on faith, an act that is commonly regarded as being opposed to knowledge. Yet, despite the apparent difficulties, no one can deny that during the past thirty centuries there has been put forth a considerable number of doctrines and writings having the name of theology, and purporting to express a knowledge of God. How is this evidence to be treated? That will depend upon the point of view adopted. From the point of view of the materialist and naturalistic humanist, these doctrines are not, in any valid sense of the term, knowledge. They must be fictions elaborated by a schizophrenic psyche to compensate for lack of adjustment to the 'real world' of experience; or they may be *apologia* for certain subjective opinions held as worthy of belief. The naturalism of materialists commits them to an external view of both religion and theology; they must regard both as psychological, social, or historical phenomena, which should be treated like all the other data of anthropology, for example, taboos or infanticide.

On the other hand, there are also many sincere adherents to the Christian faith who, from their point of view, are deeply mistrustful of these theological attempts to apply the powers and activities of human reason to matters of Christian faith and teaching. For many of these, it is not a matter of merely temperament or subjective preference that they consider it dangerous or even sacrilegious to apply rational analysis to the mysteries of faith; they have definite theological grounds for rejecting (paradoxically) the exercise of reason in theology! For example, there is a Protestant theological tradition from Luther down to Karl Barth which eschews any attempt of reason to explicate the doctrines of faith, and so to elaborate a Christian theology in that sense.[1] For these theologians, not only is human reason limited to the order of nature (upon which all are agreed); but the order of nature (and, consequently, human reason also) is so totally depraved that it is completely opposed to the order of faith and grace. Indeed, their relation is not one merely of opposition, but rather of mortal conflict, since the very presence of reason (corrupt nature) marks a contaminating influence for faith. From this point of view, grace does not heal and remove the corruption of nature which resulted from original sin; it cannot illuminate reason so as to enable it to co-operate with faith, and the dichotomy is complete. A man may hold to God by faith, but this act has nothing to do with any exercise of his rational powers; or he may exercise his reason to arrive at knowledge, even about an ultimate being and first cause; but such knowledge is worldly and depraved, and has nothing to do with the God of faith.

From both these points of view, then, theology must be rejected. But there is another possible attitude, which I take to be more in agreement with the Episcopal and Anglo-Catholic tradition represented in the Guild, so that it would be worth while to discuss the meaning and function of theology from it. Instead of an irreconcilable gulf between the orders of nature and of grace, may there not be the possibility of a redemption of nature itself by grace? [2] The crux of the two divergent views may be found in the different meanings given to the terms nature (worldliness) and grace (other-worldliness). If the reformed theologians, arguing from the corruption of nature, insist that nature can never be anything but corrupt, even when under grace, then grace may cloak a man like a mantle and affect his salvation without changing the total depravity of his nature, though it does alter profoundly the character of his works. This would seem to mean that grace redeems a man's soul without healing his nature; and that his soul ultimately enters heaven, leaving behind as incurably worldly his still corrupted nature. This dualistic view of nature and grace seems to have some likeness to dualistic views in modern philosophy, and to lead to equally disastrous consequences of both a theoretical and practical nature.

In contrast with this theological dualism, there is what might be termed the ontological view, which also accepts the corruption of nature; for it could not do otherwise without denying original sin. But the difference is that nature is not necessarily identical with corruption, for nature may be redeemed by grace from its fall, and saved. As St. Augustine never tires of repeating, nature was created good, and became depraved only by an act of man's will, turning away from God to love created things more. Thus corruption or worldliness is not an essential aspect of nature, but is nature shaping its course, or rather, attempting to shape its course without God, for it can never really do so apart from Him. But nature when healed by grace may be in the world but not of it; and then it is no longer in opposition to the order of grace and other-worldliness but in conformity. This means that man's whole nature is saved; not his soul alone. It may seem strange to be asserting that our creed does not teach the salvation of men's souls, but that is precisely the case. Do those who emphasize 'saving men's souls' forget the article of the resurrection of the body, or are they merely using the rhetorical device of synecdoche? If any further point need be made in regard to the two views of nature, is it not one of the central truths taught by the Incarnation, that through that perfect union of the two natures, human and divine, subsisting in one Person, no case of human nature is necessarily corrupt but may be redeemed by grace? Thus there is no final and irrevocable gulf set between the order of nature and the order of grace; but the former may be assimilated to the latter. That is, because the Son assumed the human nature, we with our human natures may thereby be healed and assimilated to the order of grace. And what is true of man's nature in general holds also for that aspect which we call rational; and this should throw light on the possibility of a use of reason to explicate the teachings of faith; that is, on the possibility of theological knowledge, in the Christian meaning of the term.

While this ontological view may serve to provide for the possibility of theological knowledge as contrasted with the dualistic view of nature and grace, still it does not serve to convince the naturalistic humanist, who is not willing to accept any reality beyond what can be directly observed. Against this rejection of all principles of the Christian faith, theology cannot claim to provide 'scientific demonstrations'; but it can offer persuasive arguments, and it can also show that the implied or expressed metaphysical assumptions of such a view are inadequate, and thus open the way for such a thinker to move forward to a recognition of the necessity for accepting the doctrines of the faith.

With this rather lengthy introduction as a background, it is now time to turn to a discussion of theology—that is, of Christian knowledge of a subject matter surpassing our natural powers of knowledge. This will involve a consideration of the relation of theology to other kinds of knowledge and their subject matter —theology should properly occupy the position of queen of the sciences—and thus we shall be led to a consideration of theology in practice—its relevance for man and his experience.

Theology, as its name implies, is a kind of knowledge that treats principally of God as its subject matter, and also of created things in so far as they are referred to God as their source and end *(telos)*. But it is immediately necessary to distinguish this knowledge from two other kinds closely associated with it, and often confused with it. Thus Maritain distinguishes three wisdoms corresponding to three kinds of cognitive illuminations concerning God as an object of knowledge.[3] First, the science of metaphysics, in its search for the first cause and principle of the world of observable things, is led by the natural light of human reason, unaided by the assistance of the light of faith and revelation, to rise from visible, changeable things to recognize the existence of God as well as His perfection, simplicity, and real distinction from the world. Such knowledge is usually termed natural theology, because it is based on a consideration of the effects of God found in creation, and leads to an analogical knowledge, veridical, but indirect and limited by the nature of human reason.

As historical examples, we may point to such metaphysical treatises as Plato's account of the Good, Aristotle's theological treatise in Book Lambda of the *Metaphysics,* or Plotinus' discussion of the One. More recent examples might be cited, but they might fall under the objection that their writers could not escape

some acquaintance with Christian doctrines. Even a natural theology like Spinoza's might be subject to this objection. But Plato,
unaided by faith and revelation, arrives at the Idea of the Good
from the fact in creation that men can have the experience of at-
taining an insight into an intelligible form or principle of
changing, visible things, because there must be a cause of the being and intelligibility of things, just as in the visible world the
sun is the cause of the existence and visibility of sense objects.
Similarly, Aristotle argues from the observable fact of change in
the world to the necessary existence of an unchanging, complete
actuality to account for the unceasing process of change and ac-
tualization.

Such treatises represent the highest effort of the human mind
toward wisdom, i.e. a knowledge of the first cause and principle
of all that is. These are efforts to comprehend the infinity of being, and to envisage the highest formal object of the intellect.
Small wonder that they fall short of this object, and that they require to have definite errors and shortcomings corrected and sup-
plemented by a higher light of knowledge. Thus natural theology
can establish a necessary essence as a final principle; but God
reveals Himself as primarily an act of existence: 'I am that I
am.' [4] And natural theology may demonstrate the unity of this
principle of being; but God reveals Himself also as a Trinity of
Persons.

This brings us to the second kind of wisdom, depending on a
higher light than natural theology. This might be termed Christian theology, or theology proper, since it derives its principles
from the light of a higher knowledge, namely God's knowledge
in so far as it can be revealed to men. To use Thomas Aquinas'
example,[5] there are two kinds of sciences: one which proceeds
from principles known by the natural light of the intellect, as
arithmetic, geometry (and natural theology). But there are
other sciences which proceed from principles known and established by the light of a higher science, as optics proceeds from
principles known in mathematics. So theology proper is a science
in this way, because it proceeds from principles known in the
light of a higher science, namely, God's knowledge of Himself.
So just as the science of optics, for example, accepts the prin-

ciples given to it by mathematics, so theology believes the principles revealed to it by God. There is this obvious difference, of course, that while the mathematical principles may come to be comprehended rather than merely accepted by the physicist, the principles that are revealed cannot be comprehended but must be believed. This implies a healing of man's fallen nature by faith and grace, so as to bring his natural powers in conformity with an order of truth above the created order. Is it not really one thing to which we refer when we speak of illumination by a higher light of knowledge and a healing of fallen nature by faith and grace? As St. Augustine expresses the same point: 'The lessons of instruction can only be seen as it were by their own sun, i.e. God.' [6]

It must be noted, however, that we are dealing with something quite different from the application of human reason to the data of faith. It would be a monstrous procedure to submit the truths of revelation to judgment by the light of human reason and knowledge, and to subordinate theological wisdom to the purely philosophical. Such a procedure would give not the wisdom of theology proper, but at best only the wisdom of natural theology or at worst the views characteristic of positivism and humanistic naturalism. Rather, before human reason can operate at the level of the wisdom of theology proper, it must be enlightened and strengthened by the divinely revealed truths of faith, so as to be in a measure lifted up to a proportionality with the uncreated truth which is the object of such knowledge. It is just this which was lacking to Plato and Aristotle, however sublime the heights they reached in natural theology; and it is just this illumination higher than the light of human reason which was present to Augustine and Aquinas, for example, enabling them to correct and complete the wisdom of the Greeks. And if this light is once lost, the theologian may retain all the systems of propositions and the analytical machinery of conceptual organization, but the life has gone out of it leaving only a dead body; he is no more a theologian than a corpse is a man.[7] And since the theological wisdom of the great figures in our tradition can be handed down to us only in the form of books containing these systems and concepts—in short, only the dead bodies of their illumination—we are quite rightly distrustful of them, as such. But illumination and wisdom are, properly speaking, only in a living spirit—not in a book or system of concepts, though the latter may be indispensable aids to the human spirit. Consequently, should not our criticism be directed against ourselves if these remain dead for us?

We have briefly distinguished the wisdom of theology proper from that of natural theology; it should now be distinguished from another kind of wisdom which is not properly theological. Just as we have seen that beyond the light of natural theology there is the light of theology proper, so beyond that of theology proper there is the light of supernatural grace, which Maritain calls a mystical knowledge of God.[8] It transcends the concepts and propositions of the theologian to attain a direct fellowship with God, as far as this is possible in this life. For this, an adherence to the principles of revelation by faith does not suffice, but there is required in addition a perfection of faith by the gifts of the Holy Spirit. The vision of the saint and the true Christian mystic provide the clearest examples of this wisdom and love, but it is not confined to such a few; the little child and the devout though illiterate peasant woman may receive the blessing of this gift, as well as the most learned theologian. This is the light of a person in a state of grace, in the fullness of the Christian life, and is the perfection and goal of our striving.

Now that these distinctions have been made, let us return to a consideration of theology proper—or, more specifically, to a discussion of the problem how human reason, even when enlightened by faith and revelation, can function together with that faith. How can terms and concepts, borrowed from their use in connection with created things and human knowledge, be employed in connection with revealed truths, without a complete distortion of that very truth they are intended to express? Yet we make use of our terms and concepts to express this very fact about things divine. St. Augustine states this point with his usual clarity and force: 'Have I spoken of God, or uttered His praise in any way? Nay, I feel that I have done nothing more than desire to speak; and if I have said anything, it is not what I desired to say. How do I know this, except from the fact that God is unspeakable? But what I have said, if it had been unspeakable, could not have been spoken. And so God could not even be called 'unspeakable,' because even to say this is to speak of Him. Thus there arises a curious contradiction of words, because if the unspeakable is what cannot be spoken of, it is not unspeakable, if it can be called unspeakable.' [9]

The traditional answer to this paradox, one used with high sublimity by Augustine himself, is to distinguish between the types of signification of terms, and to refer predication in theology proper to the analogical type of signification. Even though this point is doubtless familiar to many members of this audience, it may be well to give a brief restatement, in order to recall the necessary distinctions. This requires carrying along in our discussion, at the same time, two distinct orders: the order of signification and knowing; and second, the order of being, which the first order expresses and reflects more or less exactly. First, there is the equivocal use of terms, when a given term is used to signify things whose forms differ in both species and being, in both concept and nature, so that it is quite accidental that the same term should be used for both, since there is no relation in the form or nature of the things.[10] For example, the term 'jack' may signify a person, a mechanical device for lifting, or (formerly) a slang expression for money. For the nominalist, who views all things as unrelated entities, completely *other* in their individuality, and sharing in no common essence or nature, all predication must be equivocal; and the terms we use are reduced to convenient tags, because the sameness they seem to indicate are merely fictions, not *logoi*. Sameness of term does not imply sameness in the order of being.

The second type of signification is the univocal use of terms.[11] Here the same term is used to designate several things because their forms are the same in genus, or difference, or species, or properties, and therefore in being also. These examples will illustrate:

(1) generic sameness: animal predicated of man and dog;

(2) sameness of specific difference: 'powers of sensation' predicated of man and another animal;

(3) specific sameness: man predicated of Socrates and Plato;

(4) sameness of accident: weight predicated of man and stone. Here sameness in the order of signification implies a corresponding sameness in the order of being.

The third kind of signification is the analogical use of terms.[12] Here the same term may be used to designate several things because their forms are in one way the same and in another way different; a sort of mean between equivocation and the univocal use. For example, in theology we say 'God exists,' i.e. use the term *existence* to designate God's mode of being. But this term is taken from ordinary human usage and the experience and knowledge we have of existence in ourselves and other created things, so how can it be used to designate an uncreated order of being? Must this be a case of purely equivocal predication? If so, it is meaningless to use the same term, and the proposition is futile and non-significant. On the other hand, can the term existence be used univocally? This would imply a sameness of form and being which would reduce the uncreated to the created order, and do equal violence to the attempted signification.

There remains, then, the possibility of analogical predication of such a term as existence, implying that the two modes of 'existence' are in some way similar in spite of their manifest differences. But again we must be careful to distinguish between the kinds of analogical signification.[13] First, is the analogy of attribution, where the same term is predicated of several things because of their relation to some one thing. For example, to use Aristotle's illustration,[14] the term 'health' may be predicated of a living organism (animal) because it is the subject of health; of medicine, because it is the cause of health; or of blood pressure, because it is a sign of health. The common character signified by the term health is, properly speaking, possessed only by an animal; so it is merely attributed by the mind to the others, because of their relation to health as cause or sign. From the point of view of the order of being, health signifies a property of animals alone and may be used only univocally; but in the order of signification the term is attributed analogically to the others; the meaning signified is univocal in being, though analogical in concept.

To return to our example, is 'existence' predicated of God by analogy of attribution? This would mean that existence is properly predicated either of created things, and merely attributed by the mind to God, without any proper basis in the order of being; or that the term is properly attributed only to God, and the world, in Parmenidean fashion, becomes illusory.

A second type of analogy is the analogy of inequality. Here the same term signifies a common character possessed by several subjects or participants in the same way, but in different degrees of perfection or completion, or under different conditions of being. This is merely a way of viewing univocal predication from the point of view of the order of being, and is related to its discussion above. For example, 'animal' is predicated equally (univocally) of man and dog; 'but though they are equally animals, yet they are not equal animals.' [15] Similarly for sensation, when predicated of man and another animal, or the predication of any form of its many participants, provided that degrees or inequalities of participation in that character or perfection are possible.

In all these cases, in the order of being, the different degrees or kinds of perfection give rise to a certain proportionality between these participations, and hence to a kind of analogy in being. But in the order of signification and knowing, the form or concept is one in definition, and in this sense univocal; so that this oneness in definition reduces this type of analogy to univocal predication. If 'existence' is predicated of God and things in this sense, then there may be a proper proportionality in the order of being, but in the order of signification we are reduced to a single concept which serves for both the created and uncreated.

There remains a third type of analogy, based on the original meaning of the term in Greek mathematics, which involves four terms and consists in the equality of two ratios between the two pairs of terms—the proportion A:B::C:D is the simplest form and prototype of this analogy. This sameness of ratios establishes an isomorphism between the two pairs of terms, or, in more modern language, an isomorphic mapping. This is the principle of all mathematical sciences of nature from Archimedes to the present; physical measurements, e.g. weight and length, and physical laws all employ the general principle of isomorphic mapping to express the intelligible form or *logos* embodied in the phenomena. Furthermore, poets in using metaphors are employing this form of analogical signification; and Plato sets up an isomorphic mapping between the state and the individual to express the intelligible form of justice. Thus this form of analogy is the occasion and principle of our insights into the intelligible form and nature of both the world about us and our inner experience. Nevertheless, here again it is the same form or relation which obtains between the diverse classes of entities, and this sameness of form means a univocal signification as far as the ratios or forms are concerned, though not in regard to the terms involved.

Thus all these types of analogy finally reduce to a kind of univocal signification; the forms are either in the same genus, or reducible to the same ratio. This would seem to indicate that we have non-reducible analogies only when terms are used to signify objects transcending any genus, rather than being confined within a genus; that is to say, in terms of Christian theology, uncreated things. In the analogies considered so far, they have been either (1) univocal in form or concept, though there was analogy or proportionality in its participation by things (analogy of inequality); or (2) the form was univocal in existence, though there was a proportional or analogical attribution of this form or concept. There has been so far an analogical relationship either in the order of being or in the order of signification, but not in both, and consequently they were reducible, in one order or the other, to univocation. We have seen how this reducibility would affect the use of the term existence when applied to God. So it appears that only a non-reducible analogy would be valid in theology, whether natural or Christian; an analogy in which there is a proportionality both in the form or concept as well as in its participation or actual being—in the order of signification and also in the order of being, so that the two orders are conformed. Let us attempt to illustrate this by our former example; when we say 'God exists,' this predication may be put in the form of an analogy of proportion: As the divine existence is to the divine nature or essence, so (e.g.) man's existence is to human nature or essence. That is, 'whatever perfection or form is analogically common to two or more beings is intrinsically or formally possessed by each; not, however, by any two in the same way or mode, but by each in proportion to its being.' [16]

It might be objected that there is no comparison or ratio between the infinite and the finite, the uncreated and the created, and consequently no relation of analogy here. But in reply it may be pointed out that the comparison or proportion is not between the terms—not between God and man—or we should be including both terms in a common genus, and there would result a generic analogy reducible to the same ratio, like those described above. But here the comparison is not between the terms but between the ratios themselves; the ratio between divine existence and the divine nature on the one hand, and the ratio between man's existence and human nature on the other. In this case there is a proportionality between the ratios, not an identity as in the case of ordinary proportions holding between created things. Our use of this example has so far served primarily to illustrate the negative function of theology, i.e. to show what is not signified by theological terms; yet an important function nevertheless. Because it shows how, in our understanding, there can be progress from univocal to an analogical signification of terms. Analogical concepts are concepts that at first were univocal and are later rendered analogical; this does not mean that we can render analogical an order of being, which in itself is not.[17] It means that the mind first makes use of terms univocally, and then discovers their analogical signification, and along with it, the order of being thus signified—thereby bringing the order of signification and knowing more into conformity with the order of being. It seems that progress in theology, whether natural or Christian, might be described in terms of the movement from univocal to analogical signification of terms.

A luminous and illuminating example of negative theology at work, pressing on from univocal to analogical significations, is found in the last three books of Augustine's *Confessions*. In spite of the inevitable mangling of his thought and expression by condensing the discussion, I am constrained to indicate his point by a single example.[18] He begins with the statement in Genesis: 'In the beginning, God made heaven and earth'; i.e. He spake and they were made. The terms 'beginning' and 'speech' are crucial.

Suppose we take speech univocally? If so, that would imply sounds vibrating in air in a temporal sequence. But time and air both involve things in motion which can be only created things, so there must have been creation before there was creation, if God could speak, in the univocal sense. Further, since time is necessarily associated with motion and hence with created things, there was no time when the created world was not. But the term 'beginning' involves time for us. What can a timeless or eternal beginning signify? Consequently, both the beginning and the speech or word, since they are prior to created things, must themselves be timeless, eternal, uncreated—in short divine; so Augustine concludes that what is signified by both beginning and speech is the divine Word, 'through Whom all things came into being, and apart from Whom nothing that now exists came into being.' (Weymouth's trans. of John 1. 2.)

Let us turn finally to the more positive aspect of theology proper, and perhaps we can at the same time illustrate theology in its practical aspect, as queen of the other kinds of knowledge. Theology properly exercises this ruling function over the practical sciences such as economics, political science, applied psychology, et cetera, because they view man in respect of one aspect of his nature only, and consequently are competent to aim only at a subordinate and partial good, while theology is concerned with his final and all inclusive good. But there is ample evidence today that as the nations and cultures have turned more from a devotion to the uncreated Good, toward a pursuit and devotion to secular, created goods; and as there has been a corresponding loss of theological wisdom, to exercise this ruling function; so there has been a futile effort on the part of mankind to find a guiding principle in these special sciences. Thus from the point of view of economics, we have, in Dorothy Sayers' words, 'that humorless, passionless, sexless unit in a vast financial system—Economic Man,' [19] whose final good is defined in terms of the means of livelihood, a definitely subordinate good in the order of means. Similarly, when political aims and activities assume the role of finality, we have the state as the final authority, with a total government to do violence to the very essentials of man's nature in the name of the power and glory, not of God, but of the state, a temporal, created entity. Similarly disastrous results occur when men seek to make an absolute of any of the other special sciences and their goods: psychoanalysis, defining man in terms of his unconscious libido; sociology, when it defines man in terms of the herd instinct; all these represent the 'present day tendency to split up the nature of mankind, and the authority which it acknowledges, into a number of distinct and mutually incompatible absolutes.' [20] So it is properly the function of theology in its practical aspect to orient man's will and his intellect beyond a knowledge and love of these partial created goods, not that they may be despised or rejected, but that they may be seen and loved for what they are—subordinated as means to an end more in conformity with the nature of man, viewed theologically, and as relative to an uncreated good rather than as themselves being considered absolutes.

It will be objected that theology herself has been in the highest degree guilty of this authoritarianism. That this has happened in our history cannot be denied. When a religious institution becomes a political power or seeks temporal goals, as something ultimate, then it also erects partial, temporal goods into an absolute, in direct contradiction to the principles of the very theology it professes. So it is really not theology that is to blame but the leaders of that institution who have lost (or never received) the perspective and wisdom proper to theology. Stated in our terms, they have attempted to operate on the basis of the univocal signification of the theological terms involved.

In contrast to our modern partial views of man and his good, let us briefly state what would be the theological view of man and his good. Now the very basis for the possibility of theological wisdom is twofold, as has been pointed out: first, the supplementing and illuminating of the human mind by the principles of faith given in revelation; and second, the analogy in the order of being defining the relation of God to the created world, so that our univocal signification of terms can be extended to their proper analogical signification—otherwise it would be futile even to employ the terms and concepts of human language. There must be a proportion obtaining between the essence and the existence of every being that is, and this proportion in the case of the divine Being must have some proportional relation to that of created beings, as we have seen. But ultimately this second basis is in turn grounded in the first, namely in revealed principles of faith; in the doctrine of creation. Romans I. 20 is the classic text for this point: 'the invisible things of God are clearly seen, being understood by the things that are made, so the unrighteous are without excuse.' And this relationship is especially clear in the case of man, who was created after the image of God. This defines man's nature theologically, and defines his proper end and perfection as well, as we shall see. The interesting point to note here is that man's complete good is explicable only in terms of a revealed illumination about his nature, understood in its ultimate terms; just as, for example, we may define man's health and the means to it only after we have been illuminated by the light of physiological science. As an illumination of man's nature by the light of human knowledge (such as physiology) is necessary for a clear conception of the good of the health of that nature, so an illumination of man's nature by the light of revelation is necessary for wisdom concerning the final good of his nature, i.e. his salvation.

For purposes of brevity, we must compress the detailed and complete theological account of man into the compass of three major themes.[21] The first raises the question: What is his essence? And as we have seen, the answer lies in the doctrine of creation. Man, since he not only is a material object but has in addition an intellect and a power of willing, is to that extent created after the image of God. As one created thing among others, it is this direct similitude to God which differentiates him specifically from the rest of created things and defines his essential humanity. The remaining aspects of his nature he shares with other created things—sensations and passions with the animals; nutrition and life with the plants; and corporeality with the clod. The more he resembles these, the less he achieves his essential humanity. But the more he turns to God and is drawn to Him, the more man fulfils his nature, which is precisely to be an image of God. This doctrine of analogical likeness is the foundation of Christian humanism, and defines his true nature, or what he is, as seen in the light of theology.

The second major theme concerns the *summum bonum* which is defined by and required by that nature—thus a good that he desires and seeks by the very necessity of his nature—and this is happiness. But man, born of carnal desire, by his fallen nature loves himself primarily and desires other things in creation in so far as he can use them to satisfy the needs of his own self-love. But the fact is that while such gratifications may all be desirable, yet none ever suffices because, by the image doctrine, his nature is capable of, and demands, a good in the uncreated order before it is fully satisfied. For created things are good only relatively, each in its own contingent way. The human error and tragedy consist in mistaking them for absolute goods. For example, a stone is good contingent upon our need to build a wall, but not absolutely; because if our need is to satisfy hunger, then a stone is evil. In like manner all the contingent things in creation may be good, provided only we do not use them in an attempt to satisfy the hunger of human nature for its ultimate good.

So when we say that 'by nature' man loves himself and other things in so far as they satisfy his selfish desires, we are referring to him in so far as he shares the nature of other created things. Now since a man is essentially human only to the extent that he is an image of God, then it is clear that in selfishly loving other things that are only a remote *vestigium* of God, he is untrue to his own essence. Consequently, to love himself properly, that is, in accordance with his nature, a man must love that perfect Being in whose image he is created; and therein alone lies his final happiness and satisfaction. Moreover if a man love in this way, he no longer loves himself with a selfish love, and can now love other things with a disinterested love, in their true relation of their being to man's own true being, and thus enjoy their relative goodness without frustration.

Seen in this perspective, there is only one sin fundamentally, and this is a turning away of our love from God to a love of created things, though this takes many forms. But it is to be noted that sin is now seen as action that is contrary to man's true nature and the laws of his welfare, just as actions contrary to the laws of man's health would constitute a sort of medical sin. Thus divine law is reflected analogically in the laws and workings of man's nature. Even punishment for sin turns out to be a direct natural consequence of sinful action, a doing violence to the inherent laws of our nature, just as illness or bodily evil is a direct natural consequence of factors or actions working contrary to the laws of our physiological nature. In respect of his theological good as well as the goods of his body, a man has the power to choose to violate the natural laws and turn away from the proper good in each case as defined by nature; but it is not within his power to escape the natural consequences of that violation. 'For that is the most just penalty of sin, that each one loses what he would not use well; i.e. that he who knowing what is right doeth it not, should lose the knowledge of what is right; and he who would not do well when he could, should lose the power when he would.' [22]

The third general theme concerns the proper object of man's power of knowing. Just as the proper object of his will is God, wherein his natural good consists, so the proper object of his intellect is also that Supreme Being which is the source of truth itself. 'By intelligence the soul is capable of truth; by love it is capable of good; its torment arises from the fact that it seeks it without knowing what it is that it seeks, and consequently without knowing where to look.' [23] Just as fallen man begins by loving goods in the created order, so he begins by knowing other created things. Thus we have a successful knowledge of much of nature and of man in so far as he shares in the nature of other created things. But this kind of knowledge must remain silent in the face of questions concerning man's complete nature and his ultimate goal and destiny. People are beginning to ask: What does it profit a man to gain a knowledge of the whole world if he lose a knowledge of himself? For in order to know himself, a man must know his essential nature, namely his likeness to God as image. Therefore, truly to know himself, he must know God.

Nor does this theological knowledge seek to evict these natural sciences, and install itself in their place; rather it completes and clarifies them by adding on a knowledge of their end and good use. To the extent that they are seen from the point of view of their more ultimate end, to that extent they are no longer fragmentary and isolated, but can be brought into relation with one another, and receive an illumination from the highest principles of all truth and all being. The light of faith provides the principles and starting point; while understanding is the middle term between faith and the *visio Dei*.

Thus theology is reason at work, seeing everything else, especially human experience, in the light of faith; and discovering the applications of the principles of faith in all aspects of our experience, so as to illuminate and convert to their proper ends what are otherwise merely secularized human efforts directed at the transient goods of this world. And just as it is futile and disastrous for man to attempt to find his salvation and happiness in economic plans, in political organizations, or at the hands of the psychiatrist, or in any of the special secular ways, apart from the wisdom given in the perspective of theology; in the same way it is equally disastrous for man to attempt to exercise his reason and attempt to know, apart from the principles of faith. In both cases, a secularized imitation of the theological doctrine will result—some partial truth and some partial good, which, since they are not seen in the light of the whole, will themselves be taken as constituting that whole; and being thus misplaced, cease to be even the limited good they might be, and become evil. How much longer shall we pursue the illusion that searching for knowledge without the illumination of the principles of faith can satisfy the demands of the human intellect; or that the pleasures afforded by an efficient technology alone can bring peace to the human spirit and, in Gilson's words, 'appease a hunger reborn with every sop that is thrown to it'?

NOTES

1. Cf. Etienne Gilson, *Christianity and Philosophy*, New York, 1939, esp. ch. I.
2. Cf. review of Gilson op. cit. appearing in *Anglican Theological Review*, vol. XXII, no. 3, July 1940.
3. Jacques Maritain, *Les Degrés du Savoir*, Paris, 1935, p. 489.
4. Exodus III. 14.
5. *Sum. Theol.* I. Q. 1, A. 2.
6. *Soliloquies*, i, 8.

7. Cf. Maritain, *Les Degrés du Savoir*, p. 501.
8. Ibid. pp. 492ff.
9. *On Christian Doctrine*, I, ch. 6.
10. Thomas Aquinas, *Sum. Theol.* I. Q. 13, A. 5.
11. Ibid.
12. Ibid.
13. For this discussion of analogy, I am greatly indebted to Phelan's *St. Thomas and Analogy*, Marquette University Press, 1941, and to Maritain, op. cit. Annexe II, pp. 821-6, and ch. V.
14. *Met.* 1003a 32ff. Cf. also Thomas Aquinas, op. cit. and Maritain, op. cit. p. 824.
15. Phelan, G. B., op. cit. p. 19.
16. Ibid. p. 23.
17. Maritain, op. cit. p. 824.
18. Augustine, *Confessions*, Bk. XI.
19. D. Sayers, *Begin Here*, New York, 1941, p. 96.
20. Ibid. p. x.
21. These remaining paragraphs are taken largely from my article 'The Medieval Synthesis' (a review of Gilson's *The Spirit of Medieval Philosophy*), which appeared in the *Virginia Quarterly Review*, vol. 13, no. 3, September 1937, pp. 470-74. They are included here with the kind permission of the Editor.
22. St. Augustine, *On Free Will*, Bk. III, ch. 18.
23. Gilson, *The Spirit of Medieval Philosophy*.

Theology in Theory and in Practice

BY HOWARD DYKEMA ROELOFS

○

THE PROBLEM OF THEOLOGY

The setting for these papers and our discussions is that there exists an extensive body of knowledge called Theology. I use the term knowledge in a generous sense, mis-knowledge being included. There is available to all of us and to others a vast amount of material in books and articles, always readable although not always intelligible, and all this material is called collectively by a single name, theology. This enables us to refer to theology, to say theology says this, theology says that, to present our own contributions within the shelter of an established science, and in all such cases to have our reference understood and accepted. This is a great convenience. The assured existence of theology gives a reality to arguments and discussions about God which otherwise they might lack. For the existence of God is, at least for some, problematic; but the existence of theology is beyond question. This having been noted, I wish to direct our attention first not to the several topics of the papers I am to discuss, but to theology itself, to its generic and essential nature.

This extensive material called theology, taken as a lump, is intended to be what it is named, a *logos* of *theos*: a systematic, intelligible account of a specific subject, God. This *logos* of *theos* is in its statement the work of reason and claims to be knowledge. As such, it should fulfil two requirements. First, theology should be accurate about its proper object, God: it should be *true*. Second, theology should be significant for us: it should have application. These may sound like severe requirements. Yet they are no more than the ordinary ones to which the humblest science is held accountable. The difficulty is not in them, but in fulfilling them.

How can that be done? What is required for theology to be, in fact, what in name it claims to be: systematic, significant knowledge of God? Three elements are involved.

1. There must be primary data which theology starts from and with. Once started, theology can itself search for and obtain further material; but as with any science, a start is made with something not yet theology, and out of that something, with developments and additions, the science proper is made.

2. In this making, a language is developed, the language of theology. This language must be at once appropriate to its object, God, and appropriate to the aim of theology, systematic exposition, intelligible and significant to us.

3. Theology requires a method of verification, that is, criteria and procedures for testing its own results. As in the case of its language, a double reference is here involved. Criteria are needed to determine, with respect to God, whether the teachings of theology are true; with reference to us, whether they are in such form as to have application to men.

All this I fully realize is very elementary. It can be said of the *logos* of any subject. In fact, it is true of every successful science from astronomy to zoology. In each can be found the three elements just specified: primary data; an appropriate, specialized language; a method of verification and application. These are to be found, of course, not as separated, distinct building blocks out of which the science is composed. But these three elements, related and inseparably interwoven, are yet distinguishable in each science. Are they present in theology? As far as form and purpose go, theology is like any other science. But the similarity seems to extend only to form and purpose. If the similarity extended also to the performance of theology, we should probably not have had these papers read to us, certainly not the kind of papers that were read, and not the kind of discussions we did have.

It is in performance that theology falters. There is not achievement so clear and definite as to be beyond reasonable doubt. It is criticisms and denunciations that are specific and popularly accepted. From some of its critics, we who are concerned for theology can learn much; and to do this we need to be systematic in understanding what is said, for the critics are many, they say different things, and they do not always agree among themselves. To help us, I propose the following classification. Theology itself is subordinate to religion, and the basic division among its critics is found, I think, not in what they allege against theology, but in their attitude toward religion. The *fundamentum divisionis* I shall use is whether the critics accept or reject religion as genuine, of high import for human life. The crucial distinction is not between those who believe and those who disbelieve in this religion or in that, not even between theists and atheists, but between those who recognize and are serious about the peculiar significance of religion, and those who to all religion are simply indifferent.

Of these two divisions, the second requires for our present purpose only that it be correctly identified, for although those who are indifferent to religion are a major problem for the Church, they have nothing of importance to say about theology. Not that they say nothing—indifference does not keep people from talking. These people are worldly wise, indifferent to God, greatly concerned about themselves and the world they live in, and they often find it convenient to speak in a polite way about both religion and theology. On occasion they may profess a readiness to learn what theology has to say, if only its language were not unintelligible. Or they marvel that so imposing a science has in fact so little influence on men. Or they become learned in the proofs for the existence of God, and then confess with a touch of self-pity that their hearts are unmoved. Their words are significant to us, for they touch the major ends and the major weaknesses of theology; but when used by those indifferent to religion they are just phrases picked up for an occasion. Indifference, though it leaves the tongue unchecked, closes the mind;

and ignorance is not itself a good teacher. What is important for us is that having correctly distinguished these people, we shall not be confused by their words. Terms like atheist, agnostic, humanitarian, religiously minded, and so on, are easily said; and those who at bottom are indifferent readily apply any of these terms to themselves as they find it convenient, precisely because they are indifferent. The genuine atheist, the militant atheist as he often calls himself, is anything but indifferent to religion; and we should not confound him with those who are.

We are now to consider those who recognize the importance of religion and yet reject theology. Their rejections and criticisms of theology are religiously founded. That is why they can teach us so much. What do they say? From one group comes this criticism: the failure of the arguments for the existence of God, a failure after centuries of effort, is itself evidence that the enterprise is wrongly aimed. There is no God. The continued identification of religion with a nonexistent object stultifies religion at its best, and at its worst makes it vulnerable to perversion and abuse. The remedy is to promote a religion without God and, in particular, eliminate completely that false science, theology. This is the attack by the atheists. A second attack is made by those theists who deny the possibility of theology because they are convinced God's transcendence puts Him completely beyond the grasp of human intelligence. These deny not its object, but the language theology uses; of God nothing can be said. This I regard as the essence of religious obscurantism. Finally there are those who question neither the object nor the language of theology, but its relevance. God exists, He is to be known and loved, and for this the heart is enough. Rational knowledge of God may be possible but it is superfluous. The diligent pursuit of it, the self-flattering possession of it, easily become that superfluity of naughtiness of which the apostle warned. These people, earnest, devout, and good, disregard or forget the final phrase of the first great commandment, that we are to love God 'with all our minds.' These are the sentimentalists in religion. Atheists, obscurantists, sentimentalists, these are the religious critics of theology; and it is their criticisms that merit our most careful consideration.

Two items are now to be added. The first is that these three groups do belong together, not because they reject theology, for the grounds of rejection vary and thus distinguish them as three, but because their rejection of theology is made from within religion. To this the atheists seem the exception. We need to be a bit clearer about atheists than we sometimes are. Atheists deny the existence of God, not His importance, let alone the importance of religion. In fact, it is because of their positive concern for a specific kind of religion that they are so emphatic that there is no God. This first deceives and then bewilders many Christians. They learn that certain people are avowed atheists, the rigidly orthodox Communists, for example; and then they are astonished to find that these people have a religion. On the other hand, these same Christians can hardly be persuaded that among those busy with 'good works,' often with good works initiated and supported by churches, are some who are in plain fact atheists. Yet that is the case. The issue presented by atheism within religion is in modern times and among us Occidentals definite and precise. It is the issue of sovereignty. The existence of God is an insurmountable obstacle to making man, individually or collectively, the sole standard of goodness, the supreme object of worship. Precisely that, however, is the mark of the religion of the atheists at its best. At its worst, a derivative of man, humanity, the proletariat, or the state, is treated as sovereign. In any case, God stands in the way, and the atheist sets out to remove Him. Now argument alone can prove the nonexistence of God even less than can argument alone prove His existence; and yet atheism, in my opinion, relies more heavily on argument than any other form of religion. Arguments weak positively, however, can be strong destructively. This is true of the arguments of atheism. Theology, far more than religion, is concerned with argument. Thus the challenge of atheism is peculiarly a challenge to theology: the argumentative assertion that there is no God is properly encountered by the presentation of rational knowledge of Him.

This, that atheism challenges theology from within religion, is the first of the two items I proposed to explain. The second is simpler. To have a genuine theology, I have said, three elements are required: primary data, an appropriate language, and a method of verification. My second item is to point out that the three ways in which theology is rejected from within religion are correlated with these three elements. Each rejection is based primarily upon the denial of one of the elements. (1) Atheism denies that theology can have any genuine primary data, for atheism denies there is God. What theology takes to be primary data, manifestations in some way or another of God, are interpreted by atheism as data for something else. (2) When God is asserted to be beyond knowledge, it follows that theology can have no language, but only a jargon, the form of a language without the sense. (3) And when the heart is held to be alone sufficient for true religion, it follows that theology has no relevance, the question of its truth, no significance. We have now discovered a pattern within religion in terms of which three types of religion, three elements constitutive of a genuine theology, and the three most important attacks on theology, are all distinguished and related.

My assignment was to put together and interpret our papers and our discussions. For that a framework is needed, and the one I propose to use has now been stated. Its leading idea is the distinction that theology is at once a science with problems and a problem in itself. As a science, theology has a formal structure; and this structure provides also an outline of the problem of theology. Further, the three elements common to the structure and the outline—primary data, language, and method of verification—are each the focus of attacks on theology made from within religion. I did not come to this meeting of the Guild with this map of theology already in my mind. I discovered these distinctions and their multiple relations in my almost desperate endeavor to find a common theme in the papers and discussions, and a principle that would clarify what to me were perplexing ambiguities. I have been driven, and in a sense inspired, to make an independent and *ad hoc* analysis of theology as a science. I have just given not an exposition but a narration of that analysis. Its utility is now to be tested.

THE PRIMARY DATA OF THEOLOGY

Every science finds materials with which it starts, and out of which the body of scientific knowledge is derived and developed. What are the primary data of theology? These data are to be found as some aspects of experience; they *are* elements or aspects or bits of experience. Of course they are. What else could they be? This obvious truth—that the primary data of theology are to be found in experience—should not have its obviousness overlooked or forgotten; or its emptiness either. Otherwise we succumb to those who so often in modern times assert with an enormous panoply of profundity that the knowledge of God must be found in terms of human experience. If that is certain, it is not profound; for its certainty can be no more than this: if we infer God from a flower, we start by seeing the flower; if God himself speaks directly to us, and in our own language, too, we start by hearing words; in both cases the start—the seeing and the hearing—is a human experience. Certainly. Difficulties arise, I do not say profundities are uncovered, when we try to specify the religious experience. Some of us call it 'that weasel word' whenever it is used in a religious context. But why is the word 'experience' a weasel word in religion? It does not have that connotation in chemistry. Small wonder, for in chemistry the word is seldom if ever used. Whoever heard a professor of chemistry announce that chemistry is founded on the reality of the Chemical Experience? Or a professor of astronomy assert that his science is founded on the reality of Astronomical Experience? It simply is not done. Yet these sciences do in fact begin with experience, with experiences that can easily be specified. Men see the sun, the moon, the stars; they see the sun rise, move to high noon, descend to sunset; they feel the sun's warmth. These items, and others of their kind, provide the primary data of astronomy; and they certainly are human experiences. Yet we do not call them that. Why not? Take the phrase, men see the sun. The seeing is a human experience, an item in the life history of a subject; but the sun is the sun, the object seen; an item in the heavens. The transition to object is standard, uniform in essentials if not in details. Hence, if an astronomer should say that astronomy begins with perceptions, or even that astronomy begins with human experiences of the sun, moon, and stars, no one would say, 'what do you mean?' The phrase, 'experiences of' would be heard; sun, moon, stars, those objects in the heavens, would be understood. But let anyone say theology finds its primary data in religious experience, then at once it is asked, what do you mean by religious experience, and what exactly is it?

We regularly asked those questions in our discussions. No paper had for its title, 'The Primary Data of Theology,' but the subject itself was persistently before us; and the phrase 'religious experience' frequently was heard. With equal frequency some of us objected. For ourselves, we said, we were Christians, accepting and believing the Nicene Creed, the whole of it, yet never had we had a 'religious experience.' One or two of us were heard to mutter, with grim determination, that we never would. Yet the others were unshaken: no religious experience, then no religion, and, *a fortiori*, no theology, was their position.

The opposition of the two views seemed direct and mutually exclusive. Yet distinctions were made and accepted. The absolute *fons et origo* of religion, that experience, whether of the race or of an individual, before which there was no religion, is not here up for discussion or search. The origin of religion is no more an empirical question than the origin of language. It was made clear to me, at least, that this is not the result of mere lack of historical data. It is rather that to ask in the literal sense for the origin in time of language is not to ask a genuine question, it is to display one's ignorance of the nature of language. For from the nature of language, this can be said about its origin. Man can begin to speak when he has something to say, and not before; and man can begin to have something to say when he has a language, i.e. some vehicle of communication, and not before. This is not the chicken and the egg problem. If we waive for the moment the question of where the chicken came from, a chicken *qua* chicken can *be*, though there is no egg; and vice versa. But the situation as regards language is as stated above; and the case of religion is the same. Religious experiences are possible to men already religious; and men acquire religion from religious experiences. Neither can be the absolute origin for the other, since it requires the other for the first to be. The question of historical origin is, then, not to be simply dropped; it is to be seen as a misleading question. Granted there was a time when man did not exist on the earth; granted he now does; it is also and more importantly true, as Mr. Myers pointed out to us, that when in the time order man is found, it really is man that is found, man complete, using a language and having a religion. The question of the primary data of theology is not the question of the origin of religion.

Our discussions clarified a second item. Without prejudice to the genuineness of religious experiences, it was agreed that they do not seem to be essential in the life of each individual. The Church, through its teachings, sacraments, and corporate life, seems adequate to initiate, inform, and sustain religion in some men. We who proclaim, a bit too boastfully I suspect, I being one, that we have never, never had a religious experience regard the Church, under God, as the source of our religion. No scholar-churchman likes to be found questioning the adequacy in principle of the Church. But when the Church is thus credited with sufficiency, upholders of religious experience naturally claim that their opponents are actually having a 'religious experience' every time they receive the sacrament. The rejoinder is that even if they are, it is not the 'experience' that is important, but Christ incarnate in the elements of bread and wine. At this point it should be apparent that instead of a discussion, there has been a digression. Discerning the real presence of Christ in the Eucharist is for a devout Christian a completion and a culmination, dependent on his whole religious life. It is primary in importance; it is not primary in the sense of elemental material. It settles nothing as to the primary data of theology. Calling it a religious experience may be legitimate, but the meaning of the phrase is then no longer the one with which we started. What was that meaning? How is it related to our proper question, the primary data of theology?

Functionally, religious experiences should do for theology what the relevant experiences of common sense do for any other science, establish the existence of an appropriate object and give

some information about it so that the science has material to
work in and with. In this case the appropriate object is God.
But when instances of religious experience are described, what
is ordinarily given first place is the emotional tension and release
of the subject. A religious experience gives a thrill. This aspect
can indeed be established by the accepted canons of evidence.
Thrills are certainly thrilling to those who enjoy them; and to
some persons the significance of what they call a religious experience is precisely the thrill—'such a wonderful experience.'
Emotional tension, awe, and wonder are obviously appropriate
when the object of the experience is God. Yet thrill is not a
form of cognition, and what we are after is knowledge. This is
not to say that information is religion. It certainly is not. But
blind emotion is not religion either. All sorts of objects—a cold
draft, the devil, a cocktail—can on occasion thrill us; and to be
thrilled by them is not to have an experience that can provide
primary data for theology or religion. Yet the emotion by itself,
and considered as an experience, gives no sure discernment of
its object. That is why religious experience is so vulnerable to
attack on the part of the atheist, and why the very phrase has
become objectionable to theists whose faith has not dulled their
capacity for skepticism. Going to religious experience has the
specious appeal of providing religion with a firm basis in experience, an empirical basis, in a superior sense, and is supposed to set religion firmly on its feet as real. It is an empirical
fact that these experiences are experienced. But that does not
settle the question whether their attestation of a religious object
is genuine or specious. Emotion is present in all cases, and by
itself provides no answer. Yet to confound the genuine with the
specious or the specious with the genuine is no answer either.

A different approach is to examine an instance of a religious
experience which the Christian tradition accepts as genuine. In
doing this I do not wish it to be forgotten that we are seeking
the primary data for theology. When an ordinary Christian reads
St. Luke's account of the meeting of the two disciples with Jesus
on the road to Emmaus, although by faith he accepts the truth
of all that St. Luke tells, and even enters vicariously into the
wonder of that meeting, still it is an account to him of what

happened to others. What about those two disciples? Suppose they, too, did not meet Jesus but rather had heard of others who had met him, heard and believed. This cannot go on indefinitely. Religion cannot be based on a story of a story. It then is itself but a story. St. Luke himself tells us earlier in the same chapter how the apostles regarded the reports of the two Marys. 'And their words seemed to them as idle tales, and they believed them not.' Something altered that, and it was not mere words, not for those two disciples. It was an encounter with fact: Him whom they saw, they knew to be the Lord. That meeting in its entirety, from its beginning with talk on the road, to the vanishing at the end, not simply the recognition, certainly belongs in the genus of religious experience. That is certainly how it functioned for those two disciples. That is how it has been used ever since by Christian theology.

It is important to see clearly that I am not in this requiring that St. Luke's narrative be accepted as absolute truth, beyond the touch of skepticism. Of course skepticism of this narrative is possible. It is possible that St. Luke invented the entire story; he may have reported it accurately and in good faith, but those who told it to him may have imagined it or misrepresented something odd that did happen to them. And so on and so on. Nevertheless, historically this incident has functioned as religious fact and has been used as such by Christian theology. And even the firmest unbelievers should be able to see in the content of the story that it is worthy of that use. As regards the characteristics of the genus, religious experience, this instance is authentic. That is how I propose to use it.

The first thing I wish noted is that the familiar emotional tension is there, but not as a certifying element. After the recognition, and after Christ had vanished, then 'they said to one another, Did not our hearts burn within us, while he talked with us by the way?' The genuineness of the religious experience is first established by the independent recognition of the divinity of its object, and then in retrospect it is observed that there had been present the emotion appropriate to that object. The emotion confirms; it also suggests, after the event, that they were dull of sight, since feeling responded before there was vision: but it does not substitute for cognition. Certainly those disciples, who so instantly returned to Jerusalem, did not announce their great news to the other apostles, saying, 'We have had the most wonderful experience.' They said, 'We have seen the Lord.'

Stressing this point is not disparaging emotion in religion nor suggesting theology can ignore it. In religion emotion is more than appropriate, it is necessary. Emotion is indirectly cognitive: it is chiefly from our feelings that we learn that God is holy. Emotion is essential to love and action, without which there is no genuine religion. What is thus essential to religion cannot safely be ignored by theology. The mischief for religion which comes from emotion, as mischief certainly does, seems to spring from two abuses of emotion. The first abuse is when we attend to our having the emotion, to our feeling the feel, if I may so put it, instead of to the object to which the emotion itself is directed. The other abuse occurs when emotion by itself is accepted as a sufficient witness, and as more than a witness, as sufficient by itself to constitute religion. Emotion is necessary; it is not sufficient; and emotion without cognition and without action works for the devil in religion and provides no data for theology.

To return to St. Luke's narrative, a second aspect to note is that from the beginning to almost the end, the experience has what may properly be called a common-sense object. A stranger is met on the road, conversation begins and continues, the stranger is persuaded to stop for supper and rest. In these things he is all that he should be to be real as a common-sense object, no more and no less. True, his knowledge of the scriptures is distinctly superior, and his expositions are novel yet convincing. This, too, can be assimilated to what he is taken really to be, a man, another human being. And to perceive him to be such, no special organ of cognition or feeling is required, no special instruction, no special belief, no special interpretation of the common-sense object. The two disciples saw with their eyes, heard with their ears, understood with their minds, as any other men would. And what they saw was a sensible object; heard, an audible sound; understood, intelligible communications. The presence of this common-sense object will prove to be decisive for the inherent ambiguity of theological data.

This brings us to the recognition. It is customary to say that the Lord was known to these two disciples in the breaking of bread, meaning that something in that act caught their attention, awakened memory, and opened their eyes. No doubt something of that sort was the immediate occasion of the recognition; but to accept it as both the explanatory reason and the sufficient cause is to overlook the truly extraordinary amount of instruction those disciples received as they walked with the stranger to Emmaus. St. Luke effectively retains in his narrative the vigor, the thoroughness, and the sharpness of that instruction. If it needed merely some detail of feature or gesture to awaken memory, why had not that happened earlier? Was there no peculiarity of gait, no inflection of the voice, no familiar trait of any sort displayed as they walked and talked? It is written that 'their eyes were holden that they should not know Him,' but the obstacle to vision was not in the eyes but in the mind. 'Fools and slow of heart' are the words Christ used to describe their condition. Impressed as these disciples certainly had been by the teachings and works of Jesus, their minds had got no further in understanding what He was, than that he was a 'prophet mighty in word and deed before God and all the People.' He was mighty, but still a man. As a man, He died; in seeing His death, they had seen the end of Him. They did not recognize Him in this stranger because for them there was no longer anything to be recognized: Jesus was dead and gone. At the most they were capable of observing how much this living man looked, talked, walked, and in other ways was like Jesus, the Jesus who had been. But that Jesus could be living, living because He was the Christ, the Son of God, the Word made Flesh—the mere possibility of such things was not so much not believed as not grasped, not even entertained. Those disciples needed instruction, and instruction is what they got.

That is the constant feature of every account in all the four gospels of each encounter with the risen Lord; instruction precedes recognition. Those men, apostles and disciples, were neither superstitious, nor unintelligent, nor ready to let feelings dominate judgment. They were slow of understanding, stubborn in their common sense. They were not to be taken in by visions, spirits, and such like. Confronted by Jesus they argued to themselves, 'When a man dies, that is the end of him, if seen again, it is an hallucination, a vision—and Jesus was a man and died; this, then, is an hallucination.' Of themselves they could not get into their heads that Jesus was God; it taxed the Lord to get it there. And in the nature of the case, they could not see the evidence that He was God until they had in their minds that this was possible, and made a beginning of comprehending what it could mean. In this the women were quicker than the men, and of the men, the apostles seemed to have been the slowest. It is probably true that love makes the mind more receptive than does intelligence. We tend to take for granted that an independent and vigorous mind is also open-minded. Eventually it is; but initially it is more often than not strongly resistant to facts of a new and unfamiliar order; it is so fixed in what it already knows. The apostles illustrated that, and St. Mark tells us that Christ upbraided them for the hardness of their understanding. But when once the new idea is in the vigorous mind, then evidence for it, when there is evidence, is firmly grasped, and conviction is sure.

To return to the direct consideration of what happened at Emmaus, instruction had to be given prior to recognition. What was that recognition? That he whom they had taken for a stranger was Jesus: in that common-sense object, that living man, they recognized Jesus. That is the obvious answer. I think that it is not the complete answer, and that it is only ambiguously correct. There are three defects in this answer. It is an inconsequential conclusion after the instruction they had just received; second, it makes no sense with the fact that Jesus 'vanished' as soon as he was recognized; and third, in conjunction with the vanishing, it cannot be the fact of which the two disciples are now assured and which they return to Jerusalem to report. Consider these three in order. Certainly Jesus did not have to begin with Moses and the prophets in order to tell these two disciples that their fellow traveler, whom they rather stupidly took to be a stanger, was actually their own well-known leader, still alive, escaped from death. Second, if that had been the essential fact of the recognition, how completely bewildering and upsetting it would have been to have had Jesus vanish as soon as he was recognized. These two disciples had had no doubt of the ordinary common-sense reality of the stranger; he was what they themselves were, ordinary men doing a journey on foot. To have Him turn out to be Jesus would not alter the kind of object they had taken Him to be. The puzzling thing would be how Jesus had escaped death, for they thought they had certainly seen Him die, and now here He was as alive as they were. If, then, at the very instant this stranger was recognized as Jesus, he had vanished, everything in the entire encounter would have become a puzzle, an object of doubt. Had there ever been a stranger, a real, living man? If there had been, which was correct, the first judgment that he was a stranger, or the second that he was Jesus? In either of these cases, how, where, and why had he vanished? And what to do now?—hunt for the missing body to settle the question of identity?—sleep on the matter? All these are questions, not answers; they produce doubts, not assurances. Hence, the third defect—these two disciples in such a situation do not have any news, any assurance of fact, worth an instant return journey to Jerusalem to report. Yet they did go back, they were assured, they made a report. It was the apostles at Jerusalem who still remained incredulous.

This interpretation of the recognition—the stranger turns out to be Jesus—is simply not adequate to the data. What interpretation is? There are four elements in this total situation which must be coherent with each other: (1) the antecedent instruction; (2) the recognition; (3) the vanishing of the common-sense object; (4) the resultant and persistent conviction that Jesus lived. Let me restate the fatal defect of the first interpretation. It is this: if the reality of the risen, living Lord is identified with the reality of the common-sense object, so that the existence of the latter is at once the evidence for and the substance of the former, then the vanishing of the common-sense object is the vanishing of the reality of the risen Lord. The result is mystification and bewilderment, not assurance. This is not the place and I am not the person to work out the nature of the

risen body of Christ. It may be that that question is insoluble
for us. What should be clear, however, is the function of what
I have called the common-sense object. The function of that
object is to establish the reality not of itself, but of something
other than itself. Certainly the first step is to get its own reality
accepted; but this is transitional to the acceptance of a reality
of quite a different kind, and one that in this specific case required the vanishing of what was first taken to be real. It was
taken to be a living, human body, alive and real certainly, but
humanly alive, humanly real. Now let the recognition on the
part of the disciples be precisely that this common-sense object
is not a stranger, but Jesus, their master. To say that is to identify
the reality and existence of the recognized Jesus with the common-sense object. That result is disastrous. Jesus is now alive,
yes *now;* but He will be dead tomorrow or next week, next
month, next year. As for the crucifixion, either it somehow failed
of its purpose or, by a miracle like that which was done to
Lazarus, the dead body had been re-animated. In either case
Jesus is living *now,* but soon the dying, as with Lazarus, is all to
be done again, and the next time, no doubt, it will stick. We
may if we like think that this is the truth of what happened to
those disciples; but it is certain that they did not think so. The
Jesus they recognized was Victor over death, risen to die no
more. He lived, He was real, He was God, and His reality was
not that of the common-sense object they had accepted as a fellow traveler. They had been as mistaken in the nature of their
companion as they had been in his identity. When they saw who
in fact their companion was, their error vanished, vanished completely, both their idea and its object, the stranger and his body.
If only the stranger had vanished and his body had remained,
then Jesus would have been that body, with the disastrous consequence already noted. But Jesus vanished too. Of course. There
are actually two vanishings. The first is that of the stranger. His
vanishing is really total, for he never really had existed at all.
St. Luke certainly does not intend us to understand that a genuinely real person, existing all complete, not only with a body,
but with all the other trappings of a normal human being, was
suddenly transformed into Jesus. That would have made an end

of the stranger. What a blow to his parents if they were still living! To his children if he had any, to his friends! No, the stranger, never having really existed, vanishes utterly, and leaves behind not even a problem. Then Jesus, recognized as risen from the dead, God, also vanishes from sight; and this also for the instructed disciples leaves no problem behind. It leaves a conviction. But notice how different are the two convictions consequent to the two vanishings. After the stranger vanished, the conviction that remains is that he never existed at all. After Jesus vanishes, the conviction that remains is that He now lives, has conquered death, is in fact Christ, the Lord. That is the message they hasten back to Jerusalem to deliver. They would not have gone had Jesus remained at Emmaus, they would have remained also to be with Him. But He left them; they left Emmaus; and what remained with them, never to leave, was the assurance that Christ, risen from the dead, lived.

In the accounts of the other appearances of the risen Lord, whenever emphasis is given to the presence of a common-sense object, its function is the same. It overcomes initial incredulity, it convinces that what is seen is no illusion, no ghost or spirit. But what is finally established is not the reality of the common-sense object, but of Jesus as the risen Lord; and His reality is other than that of the common-sense object. The risen Lord is ready and able to do whatever a common-sense object would do, in order to convince the disciples He is real. On occasion He eats, but He does not return for breakfast, lunch, and dinner. The conclusion to be established is never 'here is a real body,' but rather 'this is the living Lord.' The *prima facie* reality of the common-sense object leads to the eventual reality of something other than itself, in this case God.

The interpretation of the experience at Emmaus which is here presented unites in a consistent, significant whole all the essential elements of St. Luke's narrative—the instruction, the recognition, the vanishing of the common-sense object and of Jesus, and the resultant, persistent conviction that Jesus lived. It accepts the supernatural and the natural—the resurrection and the crucifixion. It makes sense of both. My chief present concern, however, is what has been learned about the primary data of theology. Such data are to be of and about the divine, particularly of and about God. Religious experiences are commonly asserted to provide such data, and I have been examining a report of a notable religious experience, with some consideration of other instances by way of substantiation. Three conclusions, I think, have been worked out.

The first is about the place of emotion in such an experience. If the object of the experience is God, then intense and peculiar emotion is appropriate to that object. Emotion is also essential to the proper religious response of love and action. Further, emotion can play a cognitive role along with the other more commonly recognized forms of cognition. But emotion by itself alone cannot certify the nature or the genuineness of the object. This was noted above (pp. 108ff.), but the point bears repetition and application. Emotion is at once essential, yet by itself peculiarly open to deception and abuse. This is a dual conclusion whose two components are complementary to each other. To forget or ignore one aspect is in result to pervert the whole. In its own development, then, theology aiming at systematic knowledge cannot with impunity ignore or leave out the emotion characteristic of religious experience. This has consequences, as we shall see, for the language proper to theology. At this point, however, it is to be noted that as theology is not to ignore emotion, religion is not to ignore not merely the will, but reason. It is fatal when the emotion appropriate to religious experience is accepted as self-warranting, self-sufficient. The inevitable result is that the attention is found to turn back upon the subject, the person having the experience, rather than remain upon the object, whose divinity alone can justify the emotion as religious. The feelings of the person having the experience are certainly real. They are, as the subject says they are, wonderful, strange, deeply thrilling. But the subject is now concerned not with God, but with himself. Theology without emotion may be dead at its birth. But the emotion of religious experience without the interpretation and protection of theology keeps open house for the Devil. To keep men from God, it is not required that they plunge into gross wickedness and vice; it is enough if they are wholly occupied with themselves. The Devil is content when well-behaved people attend the religious dances of the Indians in order to feel their own responsive thrill to the beating of drums, fast on occasion in order to feel the mysterious weakness of half-fainting, and think they are in these reaching the heart of religion. They are only upsetting the regular beating of their own. No wonder a disgust arises for the cult of the religious experience. Yet it is the cult, not the emotion, which is properly scorned. The emotion itself is essential to religion, yet not by itself, but only along with other elements.

The second conclusion is that a religious experience requires an interpretative response from the subject. In the particular case examined, the recognition of Jesus at Emmaus, the response by the disciples was itself dependent upon the antecedent instruction, specific and pointed. The 'pointing,' however, was not for any peculiarities of the subsequent 'experience'—the disciples were not coached to spot something special in the breaking of bread. What they were given was theological instruction: their minds were opened and illuminated as to the way the Messiah was to do His work. In particular, a new interpretation was presented of the recent events at Jerusalem, which they had witnessed but not understood. Then, and not until then, were they competent to recognize in this stranger the risen Lord. In general, every religious experience is a reading of a revelation: to be genuine, it must be the divine that is presented; but to be read, the subject must be religiously literate.

In one way there is nothing novel in this conclusion. It is a commonplace that God is not an object of sense, not seen by human eyes in *propria persona;* that it is the religious consciousness which sees divinity in what vision recognizes only as a part of nature; and that it is the understanding heart which knows its own thrill to be a response to the presence of God. Yet the practical consequences are frequently forgotten or ignored. Certainly the ability to read springs from a native capacity, else we could as readily teach cows to read as children. Yet instruction and training are needed to enable this native capacity to function, therefore we send our children to school. Not merely the disciples, but we ordinary people, adults and children, need instruction to bring our native religious capacities into effective action. At the practical level, it matters little whether this instruction is called theological or religious, provided it is given; but clearly it is the work of theology to work out the structure and the basic content of this teaching. For what is needed is knowledge of God and of how He reveals Himself to men: what we ourselves need is what the disciples needed and were given, instruction. On the other hand, the fact on which this is based, that religious experience requires an interpretative response from the subject, is itself of crucial importance to theology. This is best presented in conjunction with our third conclusion.

That conclusion is that in the religious experience there is always an object immediately present, what I have called the common-sense object; yet not that object but what it represents or reveals is the proper object of the religious experience. The child Samuel, who 'did not yet know the Lord, neither was the word of the Lord yet revealed unto him,' heard a voice; only after he had been instructed was he able to understand that he was hearing the voice of the Lord. In the sacrament we see and taste bread and wine; what we receive is Christ's body and blood. To make this transition, to discern the divine present in the natural, is the first function of the interpretative response of the subject, and unless the transition is made there is no religious experience. Yet it is God who then reaches us; the interpretative response to the natural object is the reading of a revelation, the reception of a divine object, not the fabrication of a deception.

What then is the function of the common-sense object? It is often asserted to be wonderful, a prodigy, even a violation of the natural order, just as the attendant emotions of the subject are asserted to be intense and thrilling beyond anything previously felt. But just as to be thrilled is not in itself to be devout, so to be a wonder of nature is not in itself to be divine. Both the wonder and the deep emotion are appropriate to the presence of the Lord but they are not that presence. The bush, burning but not consumed, is still itself a burning bush. Had others been with Moses, they might well have continued to stare at that 'great sight' while he hid his face; and then they, preoccupied with the wonder and their own excitement at seeing it, would not have heard as he did the voice of God.

The function of the common-sense object, as these examples attest, is to catch the attention, to establish genuine objectivity against the possibility of hallucination or mere dreaming, to evoke, even to compel that interpretative response which says, 'here is God present.' Finally, the common-sense object can be the symbol, the visible language of God. Yet it is the subject that makes this response, it is the subject that reads the revelation. If this response is not made, though God be present in the wonder, not He but the wonder is seen.

The eventual and proper object of theology is God. But its primary data, the raw material for its work, are presented by the religious experiences of men. To say this is correct, but it is un-informing, for it offers no indication of how the transition is made from man to God. We have made a study of an example of religious experience to determine with some degree of pre-cision its essential elements. Three were found: emotion, com-mon-sense object, and interpretative response. The first two are often offered as the essence of religious experience, since the emo-tion is commonly great and peculiar, the object a wonder. But these, neither singly nor together, can make an experience re-ligious, for neither a thrill nor a wonder of itself brings us to God or Him to us. It is the interpretative response which does that, recognizing the wonder and the emotion as appropriate to the presence of God, reading with understanding whatever reve-lation of Himself God gives. It is the interpretative response in its appropriate setting which provides theology with its primary data.

In this lies the ambiguity of these data, an ambiguity not ac-cidental but inherent. These interpretations are made by a sub-ject in the presence of a common-sense object. There is ambigu-ity at both poles. The response of the subject is conditioned by his preparation, his religious competence. It takes very little in-genuity and even less psychology to make out in any specific re-ligious experience that the subject is objectifying under emo-tional stress his own religious hopes and ideas. Not until Eli had put the idea into little Samuel's head and the words into his mouth did the child say, 'Speak, for thy servant heareth.' Certainly. Without that preparation Samuel could not have responded as he did, could not have received the words of the Lord. It is fact that fabrication and interpretation equally require preparation. But from this it follows that from the necessity of preparation, it is no more legitimate to infer fabrication than interpretation. Both are possible. The response is therefore inherently ambiguous. If we turn from the subject to the object, we find a similar ambiguity. The claim of the religious experience is that it is of an independent, real object, God. And an object there certainly is. The trouble is that there are two objects. The one is the common-sense object. The reality of this object is not denied by religion, but rather its reality, including its wonderfulness when it is wonderful, is asserted to carry or reveal the reality of another object, the object proper to religion, God. But is this other object genuine or not? Clearly the reality of the common-sense object cannot be offered as evidence of the non-reality of another object it represents or reveals. What a monstrosity of reasoning it would be to argue that because the rainbow is real, God's covenant must be fiction! Such reasoning would require that for the covenant to be real, the rainbow, itself the token of the covenant, must not exist! On the other hand, if to support the interpretation that it is a token, attention is directed to the rainbow, then what is seen is—just the rainbow. Very beautiful, too. But its beauty does not certify that it is a token of God. The 'object' pole of the religious experience is as a datum fully as ambiguous as the subject pole. That is the uneasy situation of theology. Its primary data are not simple facts, but interpretations of facts inherently ambiguous.

This is a disconcerting predicament for a science to be in. Since I am favorably inclined to theology and am technically trained in epistemology, I am tempted to point out that, after all, the other sciences, even the physical sciences, have interpretations for their primary data; that these interpretations depend upon a special competence in subjects; and that the whole external material world may be only a subjective fabrication. But the temptation should be overcome. It is true that innate ideas, or the *a priori,* or the intuitive reason, in a word, interpretation, is required for us to reach the *order* of natural *objects*. It is true that pragmatists, naturalists, and naive scientists in general need on occasion to be brought to their senses, literally, so that they may see that their senses give them no physical objects, let alone causal connections. It is true that a controversial theologian could not wish for a more handsome admission from an opponent than the braggart assertation of the logical positivists that the question of the existence of the external world is a pseudo-question, unmeaning and unreal, because, forsooth, no answer is demonstrable. Yet between all this and the predicament of theology there remains a basic difference. For whether we go from *sensa* to objects by means of innate ideas and the intuitive reason, or stay with our sensations but develop an operational language for going from one to another, in all cases we remain within nature; there is no transcendence. But God, the proper object of theology, is transcendent. The type of interpretation by which we reach God and open ourselves to Him differs in kind from the interpretation involved in reaching the objects of the natural sciences. Further, the latter is in human practice presupposed by the former, but not vice versa. There is no science of God with no reference to nature; but there are sciences of nature with no reference to God.

A somewhat better analogy is provided by ethics and aesthetics, for they also reach their proper objects by interpretations whose validity as regards independent, objective existence is frequently denied. He who asserts the existence of the stars but denies the existence of God may also deny there is any glory in the heavens, although he may admit they give him a thrill. And to convince him that he thrills to their beauty can be as difficult as to convince him that they also declare the glory of God. Yet the crucial difference remains. Beauty, whether it be in the stars or only in us, is not transcendent. Neither is goodness. I am not in this denying or even questioning that God is both beautiful and good. I am pointing out that to establish the real existence in nature of beauty and goodness is not to establish the existence of God, beautiful, good, and transcendent. Many men have found the leap from nature to God easy when they base their spring on beauty, others on goodness. It is a grievous error when

advocates for religion think that no men have made the leap
from the order of nature. Many have. But there is always the
leap. The predicament of theology is peculiar to itself. It comes
from the inherent ambiguity of its primary data. Theology has
as one of its chief problems, in a way true of no other science,
the necessity of proving the bare existence of its proper object.
Theology, ancient and modern, pagan and Christian, is bur-
dened with proofs of the existence of God. But the long history
of botany contains not the slightest effort to prove the existence
of plants. The most profound and weighty conclusions of theology are open to the challenge that they are about nothing
really existing.

But that is all that is, a challenge, a question. That the existence of God can be questioned is not equivalent either to the
certainty of His nonexistence, or to there being no evidence for
His existence. No doubt the plain man is more concerned with
the making up of his own mind about God, to believe in Him or
not to, than with the special predicament of theology. Yet if
theology is to do its own work, including bringing help to the
plain man, it must have a clear understanding of its own condition. The mere fact that we do not stumble on God as we do on
plants, the mere fact that theology offers proof after proof of
the existence of its proper object, are attested by experience and
history. It has been my endeavor to increase our understanding
of that situation by working out its genesis in the very nature
of religious experience. That done, two further conclusions are
warranted.

The first is as follows. That ordinary sciences are not under
the necessity of proving the existence of their proper objects
does not mean that they never have any problems involving existence. They often do. To resolve them they have procedures
varied and complex, but all of them include at bottom a simple,
direct test. It is the test of the second look. Does the plant you
are studying really exist? Look again. What you see twice exists.
Supporting this criterion of existence is a good deal of theory,
assumption, belief; its practical applications frequently involve
a complex assembly of other persons, other places, other times;
and there is the special complexity of evidence for the existence

of imperceptibles. But in all the mazes of scientific verification there can be found, if a little trouble is taken, reliance on the second look. In the natural sciences this test is theoretically warranted as well as psychologically effective. Reliance on it, however, does have consequences which in our day receive all too little attention. But that is a question deserving independent investigation. At the moment I wish to make clear that the test of the second look is in the nature of the case inconclusive in the field of religious experience. Many relevant yet different questions tend to blur the main point. Why are religious experiences, as they notoriously are, so irregular in the incidence of their occurrence? Is God less constant than nature in response to our questionings, or less amenable? When a religious experience comes to another and I cannot get it myself, is the fault in me or in the subjectivity of the occurrence? These are not fractious questions; they are proper, practical, and vexatious. In estimating the effectiveness of the answers theology is able to offer, it should be remembered that as the believer is often credulous, the skeptic is as often perverse. He will reject a single miracle because it happened only once, and deny the religious significance of the rainbow because it happens regularly and often. This is relevant but not conclusive as to the place of the test of the second look in theology. The crucial point is this. When a datum is essentially ambiguous in kind, a second look cannot resolve the ambiguity found in the first look; it can only reproduce it. Hence the test of the second look cannot function in theology as it does in the natural sciences. Second looks are useful; they increase the number and range of our data. But all the additional data have the same ambiguity as the first. Look again at the rainbow, and see.

This is one conclusion; the other immediately follows. Like other sciences, theology must go beyond its primary data in dealing with the problem of verification. But unlike the natural sciences, theology does not, or should not, return to the field of primary data to use whatever criteria of truth it is able to develop. The specific religious experience, no matter how precious on occasion to single individuals, is not the realm in which the great questions of religion are decided. This applies even to the ecstasy of the mystic, caught up in God. That is a culminating experience for that individual, but for the confirmation of religion it remains a primary datum. Verification of religion is to be sought not in escaping from this world to God, but in living with God in this world. Life endures, thrills last but for a short time. Ecstasy is as little a test of true religion as it is of true love.

One or two applications of these results will conclude this section. It is customary to distinguish between religious experience and revelation, and in our discussions we followed custom. It is also said that in religious experience a man finds God, in revelation, God finds man. There is also the special case, the Incarnation. Here God placed Himself, so to speak, squarely in public, so that no finding was needed, but just seeing. Each of these distinctions is based on a real difference, but for theology certain common features are equally if not more important. In the personal religious experience there is often, I am ready to believe, a kind of breakthrough from ordinary reality to reality of another kind, and the man, as he says, finds God. It is then appropriate that he give large place to the intense joy and wonder of that finding. There is a kind of reversal of this for the human instrument in revelation. There comes an interruption of normal life, and any attendant self-regarding emotion is overwhelmed by the compulsion to publish the message that comes from God. In the case of the Incarnation there was for the people among whom our Lord lived neither breakthrough nor interruption of ordinary life, nor special emotion, either, most of the time. There was a man who taught and did things. For some of us today this aspect of the Incarnation is peculiarly attractive because it is free from the emotionalism of religious experience and from the mystery of inspiration. Of course our knowledge of Jesus is based on the reports of others, but for them to hear and put down His teachings, to see and record His work, required in them no peculiar emotion, no guiding inspiration. They made a record of what was publicly and objectively said and done. Jesus, the Christ, the Incarnate Word, spoke these words, did these deeds, and in them He made God manifest to men. Thus is the Incarnation, so we think, set apart.

But this is to mistake the results of religious and theological interpretation for the primary data from which they spring. It is to forget that most of those who saw Jesus in the flesh did not recognize Him to be the Lord. It is to forget that His teachings provoked indignation, His miracles the opinion that he was possessed of a devil, and His claim to be God the accusation of blasphemy. Part of the greatness of the Gospels as narratives is that they retain all this in their presentation of the earthly life of Jesus. They faithfully preserve the belated recognition of the disciples themselves.

For the person receiving a revelation, for a person having a religious experience, and for those to whom the Incarnation presented a primary datum, those who knew Jesus in the flesh, there is a constant pattern. There is a common-sense object, there is the evocation of an interpretative response. And there is also the inescapable ambiguity. Have I found God or only myself? Is this a message from on high or the upheavings of the subconscious? Is this God or man?

It is among revelations, not apart from them, that the Incarnation is unique. It is also dependent upon other revelations in a specific respect, for they helped to develop the religious literacy of the disciples, without which no recognition of the Incarnation was possible. Religion existed long before the Incarnation and is to this day more extensive than the acceptance of Christ. Christian theology cannot restrict its primary data to the Incarnation, even in the setting provided by the religious experience of the Jews. Christian theology should include in its scope revelations that have come to non-Christian peoples. There is but one God. A difficulty does arise, however, in the use by theology of what are commonly called religious experiences, and the difficulty has nothing to do with their genuineness. If the experience is really religious, then it is of God. The defect in the religious experience is that not only is it private in its occurrence, but it usually remains so in its significance—it remains personal, individual, exclusively subjective, and the transition to corporate religious life is rarely made.

Again following custom, we used the contrasting terms, revealed and natural theology, and in each paper something significant was said of the nature of each and of their basic differ-

ences. Revealed theology accepts and is based upon what it regards as accredited revelations. It is this that makes revealed theology so open to secular attack. No matter how careful and precise it is in its own developments, it seems to the outsider to be
completely credulous as regards its initial material. Against this
stricture natural theology is said to be proof, for its data are
taken exclusively from what is known to common sense and
natural science, with no taint of revelation, no ambiguity of
meaning. The data are found by science and common sense, and
they mean what these same authorities say they mean. How, then,
it may well be asked, can natural theology have anything to say
that has not already been said? The official answer is that in these
data reason may discover implications, not alternative, but additional to the already established meanings. These implications
it is the work of natural theology to derive, systematize, and
assess. The pattern of natural theology is, accordingly, argument:
from nature there is an *inference* to God. It is granted by almost
everyone that these arguments fall short of conclusive demonstration, although they are ingenious. But the question now arises,
why make them? If the objection to revealed theology is that it
rests upon credulity, natural theology can be criticized for resting
upon a foolish taste for the superfluous. Common sense and
science tells us all that can certainly be known about nature, and
that should be sufficient. There is no need and less warrant for
trying by argument to get beyond nature. And even if the in-
genuity of the arguments makes them fascinating to those with a
cultivated taste for dialectic, the whole enterprise is in any case
religiously futile. Who ever heard of natural theology teaching
a man to pray?

The element of caricature in this summary account of the two
kinds of theology has been deliberate. It is made plausible by
treating revealed theology and natural theology as two independent and separated sciences. To question and reject that
separation was, I think, the chief result of our discussions of
those two disciplines. The natural theologian is no single-minded
logician surveying natural knowledge to see what inferences are
possible; he is not even the philosophical ontologist arguing that
contingent being requires there be necessary being. He is a the-

ologian. It is evidence and demonstration about God which he seeks. In all his seeking he has a clue. Whence his clue? That was our persistent question. An instant answer is, revealed theology, and I have found that answer recorded in my notes. It is a true answer to this extent. It can be shown in the case of specific natural theologians that they were guided in their work by religious ideas taken over if not from revealed theology, certainly from revealed religion. But revealed theology is in a similar case both as regards the theologians themselves and as regards those who received the revelations revealed theology accepts and uses. How are revelations recognized? Not how are authentic revelations sifted out from the spurious, but how is it anyone ever thinks there may be such a thing as a message from God? Unless such ideas were in the mind, there could be no understanding of divine utterances, though He spoke never so loudly and began, 'this is the Lord speaking.' It now seems that it is natural theology that prepares men to receive revelations. This, too, I have in my notes. And that all theology is dependent upon the primordial religious experience is also there recorded. Yet that, too, requires that the subject be to some degree religiously literate.

If this were a dispute about precedence in time as regards origins, it would be as trivial as it is futile. The matter of origin in time has already been dealt with. Further, the important thing in theology, as in religion, is not how one starts toward God, but how best to reach Him. Rivalry among the means is unseemly if not worse. But our discussions produced other and important conclusions. As in our examination of religious experience, so now in the case of theology, both natural and revealed, we find the necessity of an interpretative response of the subject, and this depends upon a capacity that is both innate and needing cultivation. If the image of God were not already in his heart, no man could recognize Him in nature, in revelation, or in religious experience. Equally all three mutually guide and illumine each other. What is so baffling is the extraordinary range among men of the responsiveness of this capacity. Innate capacities in fact, regardless of how they are named, are a commonplace to philosophical reflection. It is the privation of innate capacities which makes some individuals idiots. But there are men, anything but idiots, who seem to be dead to the image of God in themselves, and hence also to God. That He does not forget them, but extends to them His grace through means they are ready and able to accept is what we believe. This we affirmed and we gave instances to substantiate our belief. Yet the fact remains that there are men thus helped to whom the words 'God's grace' are an empty sound. To that we found no answer.

Another conclusion has the possibility of direct practical application. Natural theology should give up its pretension to independence. This is not a plea to abandon the endeavor by reason to read in nature a revelation of God. But that this is done with absolutely no help from revealed religion should be eliminated as completely in claim as it is nonexistent in fact. During the revision of this essay I heard an able priest preach a sermon at whose beginning he announced that he was going to start from scratch, accept nothing from revelation, and use only reason and science. At the end of ten minutes he had reached a fair facsimile of God, and the assertion was repeated that the start had been made 'from scratch.' Of course he had done no such thing, and this was patent to any attentive and reasonably informed listener. Such a sermon because of that pretension brings no help to a person perplexed with religious doubts and honestly wrestling with them. It merely soothes the complacent, and they need to be disturbed.

Revealed theology has also its lesson. It tends to be sectarian even when practiced by Christians in the catholic tradition. The remedy is not making an end of Christian theology but developing a theology in which the religious interpretation of nature, the data of religious experience and of revelation, Christian and non-Christian, are united in a single doctrine of God.

THE LANGUAGE OF THEOLOGY

The title of this section is that of Professor Urban's paper, and a substantial portion of Professor Hammond's was devoted to the same topic. No outline of these papers will be attempted by me, since the organization of each makes such assistance to their reading unnecessary. It is well to point out, however, that although this topic is named 'The Language of Theology,' we are not confronted with a literary problem about words. We are not in search of *'le mot juste'* for theological expressionism. We are concerned with the reliability and the adequacy of the meanings used by theology, on the one hand to the reality to which they refer, the divine, and on the other hand to the function of communication for which they are the instrument. Can the language of theology be at once accurate as to God and intelligible to men—that is the problem.

It may be helpful to suggest that Professor Hammond is chiefly concerned to make an analytic survey of the difficulties, Professor Urban with establishing the goals, of an adequate language of theology. I shall begin with the difficulties. God is transcendent and holy; man is of this world and depraved. The creature lacks the cognitive capacity to grasp the true nature of the Creator, and even if he could, sin would pervert what reason obtained. A counter to this difficulty is that it is theology using theology not for self-criticism but for self-destruction, for the transcendence of God and the sinfulness of man are themselves theological conclusions. I am not denying the primary facts: the transcendence of God, the sinfulness of the creature, and the consequences for man's knowledge of God. I am pointing out that imperfect knowledge is still knowledge, and not stone-blind ignorance. Instead of further arguments on this matter it is better to look at performance. It is in knowing the holiness of God that man comes to know his own sinfulness. It is not for theology to say this cannot be done. It is done. What is needed from theology is an exposition of what is involved when a man cries, 'Lord, have mercy on me, a sinner.' Not what words, but what ideas, what cognitions are to be used to present in reasonable terms this relationship of sinner, mercy, and God.

Another difficulty for theology arises from the use of faith. Man is imperfect and limited; God is supra-rational; but, it is said, by faith, perfected by divine illumination, man may believe what he cannot understand. It follows that the content of such belief will baffle theological, i.e. rational, communication. I challenge the phrase, men can believe what they cannot understand. Two meanings of this phrase are significant and true. But there is a third which is just nonsense, yet it is this nonsense which seems most commonly to be intended. The significant and related meanings are these: we can believe something to be true although we do not know the evidence required to establish its truth. There are endless illustrations of this outside religion. I can believe a man who says he was not at the scene of the murder, in face of testimony from others that he was, and I can be without evidence to prove that he was elsewhere. Here I certainly understand what my belief is—I understand what it is for a man to be at a given place, and what it is for him not to be there. I also have some knowledge of the man himself, and that is why I believe him. See how in this case faith rests upon and is ringed about with knowledge. Yet faith at a specific point goes beyond knowledge.

In a second meaning faith seems to run counter to understanding. Here I shall use an illustration from religion. It is the union in God of justice and mercy. With us men the doing of justice requires on occasion the refusal of mercy, the showing of mercy the curtailment of justice. How can God do both? We do not understand how, yet we can believe that He does. But clearly there is in us quite a bit of understanding. First, it is our understanding of justice and mercy in separation which presents the obstacle to their union. Second, there is the recognition that our grasp of justice and mercy is incomplete. Third, we have some knowledge of God's love. There are other factors, no doubt, in the motivation of belief. But certainly these three understandings function when we say of God's mercy and justice that we believe what we do not understand.

The third, and to my mind, the nonsensical use of the phrase, believing what cannot be understood, is obtained by denying the knowledge found in the illustrations already considered. Consider the statement, 'God only is holy.' Of this let a man say, I can pronounce and spell that word, holy, but to me it simply has no meaning, and if alleged evidence were offered of the holiness of God, it could not be evidence for me since I could not grasp what it was about; yet with no understanding whatever, I believe God is holy.

The proper comment to this is that he doesn't and can't. Some may think that I am rejecting rather roughly a delicate and important stage in the cultivation of faith. Really I am not. There are appropriate nonrational factors in the motivation of belief. The mind can be receptive to meanings it cannot yet take in; to the words that convey those meanings there can be attentiveness and reverence, as when a child bows his head to the Sanctus. But so long as understanding is utterly a blank, belief is equally empty.

What has this to do with the language of theology? A great deal. Faith, understanding, reason, knowledge, these are some of the terms theology most frequently uses. The clarification of its own technical terminology is a constant obligation on theology. In particular, the mutual dependence of faith and knowledge, feeling and reason, instead of their separation and opposition, could be more effectively presented than seems to be current practice. This has been a recurrent theme in Guild discussions. We, scholars and Churchmen, do not found our personal beliefs upon sheer ignorance, welcoming some admission of failure from science so that we can plunge into the mystery of religion. In our own particular fields we constantly find knowledge resting on faith, faith springing forward from knowledge. We find the same pattern in religion.

This brings us to what is probably the crucial difficulty in the language of theology, the presentation of God's attributes. Is the term 'holy,' for example, accurate about God and intelligible to us? There are several possibilities. One is that God may so reveal Himself to man that direct cognition occurs, and it is such cognition which is the source of our understanding of the term 'holy.' Holy is to God as heat is to flame, an attribute known itself in the object to which it pertains. My recollection is that this is substantially one of the theses of Otto's book, *'The Idea of the Holy.'* Professor Hammond takes the more common position that the predicates we apply to God are analogical. We have some knowledge of fatherhood at first hand, and then by analogy we describe God's relation to us as that of a father. Mr. Hammond asks what is the nature of the analogy, and finds no satisfactory answer. The analogy is neither that of being nor that of predication. To affirm that man is created in the image of God, and therefore we are warranted in going from man to God, is not as helpful in performance as in promise. In what sense is man God's image? Knowledge of the original here seems a prior necessity to understanding the copy.

I shall not carry these reflections further because I lack confidence in my notes, and the paper is available in this volume. But I wish to present one or two observations which, quite apart from Mr. Hammond's paper, are relevant to the difficulties we have been discussing.

There are difficulties of language for theology arising from the nature of its proper object, God, and from the peculiarities of our cognitions of that object. But the greater part of these difficulties presuppose some knowledge of God and have to do with the specifications and communications of that knowledge. Three persons and one God is a familiar instance of this kind. But if we say of this characterization of God, 'stuff and nonsense—there is no God at all,' we are not finding fault with this particular item of theological knowledge or with the language in which it is stated. Any and every statement about God would be equally stuff and nonsense, and all for the same reason—the denial that there is an object, God, to be known. It is when we assert that God is ineffable or that three persons cannot be a unity, that this characterization of God is itself the object of criticism. God's existence and something of His nature are now assumed to be known or grasped in some way, by feeling, for example, if not by reason. Difficulties of this sort and attempts at solutions are the theme of this present section. But difficulties also arise, independently of theology, with respect to our knowledge of any object whatever, and then on these general grounds theology is rejected. This is disingenuous and confusing. The confusion I propose to clear up.

Some men, notably some philosophers, find so much trouble in understanding how we can know an object that to escape that trouble they deny the knowing, and affirm something else as a substitute. For example, the direct cognition of any attribute is denied, but indirectly we can learn what an attribute is like: the flavor of coffee, it is said, cannot be grasped, but it can be learned that postum tastes like it, and this is of practical importance, since it teaches us to brew postum when no coffee is available. Another position is that we cannot learn what water is —no cognition of being is possible—but we can learn how to get a drink, and a drink is a wonderful experience. The application to theology is easy: 'No knowledge of God is possible and theology is a vain pretension. But religious experience can be accepted as stimulating and helpful, and the development of reliable methods for getting these experiences and turning them to account in everyday life becomes the practical problem of a science of religion.' It is plain that there is a fundamental opposition between those who affirm the competence of human reason to grasp the being and nature of objects, and those who deny it. It is plain that if all rational knowledge of objects is denied, knowledge of God is included in the denial. But it should also be plain that although God is included in the denial, nothing peculiar to Him is involved. He simply falls under the same condemnation as water—both are objects and therefore unknown.

Personally I am persuaded of the competence of reason to know objects; and with those who deny it I am ready to engage in philosophic debate. I am also ready to consider on their own merits the difficulties peculiar to theological knowledge. But the situations are different, and confusion results when criticisms of the possibility of knowledge in general are cited as though they were difficulties peculiar to theology. Theology has troubles enough of its own. If the general problem of knowledge is to be discussed, misleading connotations can be avoided by leaving out God and sticking to such situations as the experience of having a drink, and whether water or whisky is required to make the experience wonderful, and whether this can be determined without any knowledge of either, let alone knowledge of scotch, bourbon, and rye.

Returning to theology, I find in Professor Urban's paper, as I have already said, an effective presentation of the goals the language of theology should aim at. Men are religious before they are theologians, and the language native to religion is pictorial, symbolic, poetic, emotive, often culminating in songs of praise and thanksgiving. It is often dramatic, often in the form we call myth. Reflection on what is thus recorded readily generates this question: can the meaning of this religious material be restated in clearer, more systematic, and more reliable form, so that it will be intelligible and religiously significant to men in general? To do that is a task for theology. The language problem peculiar to theology is now apparent. It is to make the translation from poetry to prose, emotion to reason, the pictorial to the abstract without loss of meaning and truth. That theology must do precisely this is Professor Urban's thesis. And I wish it noted that a translation from symbolic to the literal is not set up as an objective.

Some religious language is soberly matter of fact. 'Forgive us our trespasses as we forgive those who trespass against us' is neither dramatic nor mythical in its language. The use of the word 'trespass' to cover all forms of wrongdoing may be called a metaphor, but it is not peculiarly religious. The emphasis on the poetic in religious language can, I think, be overdone, as when it is claimed that the real truth of Christian doctrine is just one sweet song of love. Yet what Professor Urban says is substantially true. Questions arise with respect to the objectives he sets up for the language of theology. I shall consider two: the first, are his objectives correct; the second, can they in practice be achieved.

Our first question is really this: are the metaphorical and emotive aspects of religious language appropriate vehicles of its meaning? Or are they at best merely decorative expressions of our feelings, at worst a fancy display of words concealing an emptiness of sense? The following considerations are pertinent. Every significant term is about something, its object or referent; and, as Professor Urban says, the first requirement for reliable meaning is that the word be appropriate to its object. The nature of the object is here definitive. This is frequently forgotten. Some people think that a description of man to be really accurate must be stated in the quantitative terms of the physical sciences. This is correct if, and only if, man himself is essentially quantitative, for words about man must be appropriate to what he is. So also with God. What He is provides the standard by which language about Him is to be judged. If God's nature is such that, at His approach to us, awe and fear constrain us, then words expressive of this are part of the truth about God. The hazard to truth is not in the vivid characterization of the awesomeness of God, but in our responding to the words rather than to Him. Usage and habit can give to words themselves power to evoke our feelings, so that we bow the head merely to the word 'holy.' But to reason from this to the conclusion that God should not be called 'holy' is unwarranted. That would be to hold that because men err, the truth should not be stated.

A second consideration makes use of a conclusion reached in Part III of this essay. What is there called the common-sense object is regularly present in every type of revelation, from private religious experience to the Incarnation. But the object revealed is other than the common-sense object in two senses: it is something else, and it is other in nature; in most revelations, it is God. The problem of describing this 'other' is not easily solved. Literal description of the common-sense object is easy. There it is, a part of the natural order, open to inspection with language developed and adapted primarily for just such objects. But what is revealed, although given to the subject, is yet received only by an interpretative response of the subject, and is in itself not an element in the order of nature. Metaphor and, at times, myth obviously are here not merely appropriate but accurate, since they preserve the 'otherness' of what they describe. A passage in St. John exposes both the problem and this solution. 'Then came there a voice from heaven, saying, I have glorified it, and will glorify it again. The people therefore, that stood by, and heard it, said it thundered: others said, An angel spake to him.' (St. John XII. 28-9.) In scriptural accounts of revelations it is notable that messages from God normally are presented in the literal language of common sense, for in these the transition from the divine to the natural order has already been made. Objects within the supernatural order are what chiefly require metaphor and myth. The problem for theology is not so much to justify their use but first to understand the meaning present in them, and then to develop a technical language adequate to that meaning. In religious myth, as Professor Urban says, the mythological is in the manner of the description, not in the matter described. It is this matter which must be preserved in theology. It is tempting to suggest that this difficult task is really unnecessary: let people grasp religious truth for themselves in the language religion naturally uses. But this is to forget that revelation comes to most men at second hand. Only three disciples witnessed the transfiguration of Jesus: it is significant for all men. How are they to understand what they did not witness, and what is first presented to them in metaphorical language? Theology should be their interpreter and guide. The language of theology, to repeat Professor Urban once more, must be at once adequate to the truth present in the metaphor, and intelligible to men. It is popular at present to exalt religion and decry theology, but my own experience is that we ordinary men need for the improvement of our religion far more theological guidance than we are given.

God, the object of theology, and God, the object of religion, is one God. Again and again Professor Urban affirms this. Both the importance of this and that it is stated in an essay on the language of theology are most readily understood by those familiar with philosophical speculations in the field of religion. In the Christian religion God is emphatically and essentially the living God, and as living He is the object of fear, awe, and love. In theology God too often and too readily becomes an abstraction. His essence may involve existence, yet this existence remains, so to speak, quiescent. Eventually a dualism results. In religion there is God, in theology there is abstract Goodness. In effect this leaves religion without a theology, and God becomes subject to an independent moral standard, the good. In philosophy this is a famous problem in the interpretation of Plato. Are God and the Form of the Good one or two? How are they distinguished, related, or united? That Goodness and God must be two is maintained by some eminent philosophers not only as regards Plato, but generally. For the Christian religion to accept this dualism is to admit that God does not possess in His own nature moral sovereignty. Not even Plato, according to Urban, did that. The ordering power of the Form of the Good over all other forms, he says, is the evidence that this Form is not an essence co-ordinate in nature with other forms, but that it is God. This is of particular interest to students of philosophy. For men generally and for Christian theologians particularly, it should make clear that theology does its work better when its language constantly makes manifest that its object is identical with that of religions, the one living good, God.

The first of the two questions addressed to Professor Urban's paper, does he correctly state the goals of the language of theology, has now been answered in the affirmative. This agrees with the course taken in our discussions. In fact we were for a time a bit too ready and too extreme in our acceptance of the use of metaphor. We needed the admonition of Mr. Wild that the use and understanding of metaphor requires knowledge that is not itself metaphorical or analogical. We must know what a hedge actually is and does if we are to understand the metaphor that divinity doth hedge a king. But when we took up the second question, are these goals practically possible, doubt and dissent were general. Professor Thomas expressed the experience of many when he said that the tragedy of theology is that in practice the translations of religion lose precisely what Professor Urban says should be preserved. To the extent that this is true, to that extent are theological writings defective. It remains possible that they could be better than they are. Second thoughts on this produced the following suggestions. Perhaps our survey of theology is too narrow. If some theology is arid, making a poor showing of preserving truths expressed poetically by the language of religion, there is considerable poetry which to my mind states with great success theological truth. And the amount of theology incorporated in our liturgy is great. How can Christ be discerned in the Eucharist? 'Faith the outward sense befriending makes the inward vision clear.' Is the flesh evil, hated of God? 'God, Who hatest nothing that Thou has made.' What is the source of evil? 'We have followed too much the devices and desires of our own hearts.' These are theological propositions. They are not all that theology can say on these several topics, but they are admirable topic sentences for further exposition. There is more good theology available to us than we realize. What we need to do is to attend to it—and if we aim at being theologians, emulate it. The 'language of religion' and the 'language of theology' are useful phrases in an important but rather narrow context. Their use should not mislead us; there are not two separated and complete languages, one religious, one theological, with translation the only route from one to the other. One of the conclusions previously established in this essay is that to receive a revelation an interpretative response is required from the subject, and his competence in this depends in part on his religious literacy. Theology functions in religious experience, and permeates its language. The really basic language problem—adequate, accurate expression of divine reality—is best left for solution in detail to theologians who are religious, and to the devout who are theologically literate.

Good theological writing is possible. But our studies in this section have also substantiated one of the conclusions reached in Part II. There the problem which is theology itself was stated, and its several aspects indicated. Let it be granted that theology is to preserve in its own language the truths religion expresses in myth and metaphor, and let it be granted that it is God's nature that requires such language. How easy it then is for the obscurantist in religion to pervert this into an admission that God is beyond the cognitive capacity of man. How easy to cite poor theological writing as evidence that the sustained pretension to knowledge of God produces only a jargon. How tempting the plea, give up trying to know, only believe. For religion to succumb to obscurantism is to make certain the victory of secularism. Yet of vivid theological writing it can still be asked, is it true? is it of any use? To those questions we now turn.

<h3>CRITERIA OF TRUTH AND APPLICATION</h3>

Two papers come under this heading, that of Professor Thomas, 'Theology and Philosophy,' and that of Professor Wild, 'Theology and Dogma.' An unusual circumstance attended the presentation of both. There was a general expectation, shared by the authors, that these two papers would be sharply opposed. The reading and the initial discussion seemed to confirm this expectation. Thus the papers in terms of their own content pose the problem of verification.

The paper of Professor Thomas can be described as representative of liberal orthodoxy. He is distressed, as all of us in the Guild are, by the indifference at the intellectual level of the modern educated man to both theology and religion. Crucial evidence is supplied by the relation of philosophy and theology. They display today not even the interaction of conflict; they simply follow divergent paths. Natural theology to the extent that it persists as a philosophic enterprise aims not at being rational but at being empirical. The proofs for the existence of God which it offers claim problematic validity only, and are subject to continued testing and revision in human experience. With this Mr. Thomas is in sympathy. But both his debt and allegiance to orthodoxy are indicated by his clear account of the limitations of naturalism in religion. It can recognize sin, but give no deliverance; it can awaken hunger for divine food, but has none to offer. It is here that revealed religion and revealed theology should function vigorously and effectively. Why do they fail? Mr. Thomas answers. They are shackled by the finality they claim for historic revelation, that which has already happened. Their very theory of revelation displays this fault. God impressed ideas on the passive minds of prophets and saints—this theory is credited to St. Thomas Aquinas—and the only activity allowed them, and us, is to reject these ideas, or by an act of will to accept them, that is, to believe them. A modern educated thinking man refuses to be passive and uncritical in religion. To him the food offered by tradition is lifeless. He needs religion, revealed religion, but he must achieve it for himself, test it for himself. Only thus can he have confidence in its truth, find it to have practical application in his own life.

The remedy urged by Mr. Thomas, like his diagnosis, combines orthodoxy with liberalism. The past is not to be excluded; it cannot be. The Incarnation is man's salvation and it happened long ago. But what happened was an event. The religious significance of such events requires, as this essay has also steadily maintained, an interpretative response from subjects. Those events, as events, are available through history to us men today. There is no necessity that the interpretation of those events made so long ago should be passively accepted by us under penalty of losing the events themselves. We men of today can and should

rethink and reinterpret those events, rethink the Bible, reinterpret the life of Jesus, rethink and reformulate the historic creeds,
using on the one hand all the resources of modern scholarship,
and on the other all the insights found in the vigorous cultivation of personal religious experiences. The result will be not
only a new orthodoxy; it will be a renewal of religion. We will
be sure of its truth and its utility, for we will have made it and
tested it in the immediate experience of living. The method is
dangerous; independent thinking always is. But the goal is worth
the hazard.

I hope in this summary I have reflected something of the vigor
and appeal of Mr. Thomas' paper. I am sure that those who read
it will be stirred in their hearts, and attracted by his proposals.
It is possible, of course, to criticize his paper at particular points,
and I shall mention one. It is true that the event called the Incarnation happened independently of the interpretations of it.
But it is not true that the Incarnation as an event is available to
us, independently of interpretations of it. We know the Incarnation only as the Gospels give it to us. What they give is at once
a record and an interpretation. Were this not so, the Gospels
would not be the Good News. For most of us, revelations are
available only as interpretations of events, these events happening to others but not to us. We can rethink their significance, re-
vise our opinion of their truth, discover new applications to ourselves, but we cannot make the revelations reoccur, and then
rethink them.

But this type of criticism does not reach the chief question to
be put to the paper of Professor Thomas, particularly in its present setting, that provided by Professor Wild. Here is the question. A rethinking of Christian doctrines is required. What will
fulfil that requirement? In particular, is the paper of Mr. Wild
an example of what Mr. Thomas says is necessary, or is it a challenge to his proposals?

That is the one question about Mr. Wild's paper I propose
to answer. I shall give no summary at all, but I shall describe
the paper and state how I think it should be read. In Mr. Wild's
paper a rational, realistic theory of knowledge is stated, and the
historic doctrines of orthodoxy are enumerated in a series of

propositions. These are asserted to be theological knowledge. Why did we take this paper to be in basic disagreement with that of Mr. Thomas? The reason was obvious and was stated. Because the conclusions reached by Mr. Wild are those of historic, catholic orthodoxy. That reason is our error. The rethinking of Christian doctrine is demanded. Orthodox conclusions are offered. Therefore they are not the result of rethinking. The error in reasoning is so bad it is grotesque. Yet it is easily made, constantly made, is, in fact, a characteristic error of religious liberalism.

We live in a changing world, as every one of us by this time should know. All around us are new discoveries, new inventions, new experiences, new problems, new ideas. There are also some old problems, persistent problems. And for these there are old solutions which have persisted. But we wish to be sure of the solutions, and we have the most reliance on what we do ourselves. We put to one side the old solutions, and we attack the old problems with new energy, new experience, new ideas. All this is to the good. But at this point all too often we simply go off the track. We let association of ideas, the repetition of the word 'new,' a desire for novelty, and other such causes produce in us delusion that since the thinking is new, the conclusion must also be new, that is, different. In that delusion we turn away from renewed affirmation of traditional solutions, assuming that they can be only the passive repetition of old stuff, outmoded, inapplicable to the world of today, false. One way to dispel the delusion is to make its implications specific and baldly plain. This I shall now do in the present instance. Mr. Wild's paper is certainly orthodox. How did he come to write it? We know he is a scholar. Are we to believe that in writing this paper he deliberately disregarded his own competence? His own religious experience? Did no thinking of his own? That he simply took down some handbook of medieval theology and from the index derived a series of orthodox dogmas? We know the contrary.

How then are we to read his paper? I suggest that the paper of Mr. Thomas be read first. Then read that of Mr. Wild as an example of a diligent endeavor to rethink Christian doctrine.

Is it really so astonishing that the results reached are in agreement with historic formulations? I do not think so. I find rather
that this is new evidence that those historic formulations are true.

CONCLUSION

But are they true? How are any conclusions in theology certi-
fied and confirmed? That question has not been answered. Theology, so far as I can discover, has no procedure, in the usual
sense of that term, for demonstrating the truth of its own conclusions. By criteria of consistency and adequacy, using analysis and
argument, theological conclusions can be shown to be correct
with reference to the religious material from which they start.
But the question of verification carries us beyond correctness to
the truth of religion itself. If there is a God, if there are revelations of Him, then, though those revelations are first stated in
metaphor and myth, theology can work out knowledge of God.
But can theology remove the 'if'? Not by repetitions of the primary data; they are and remain inherently ambiguous. Not by
revising the language of religion. Not by its own independent
efforts. What, then, is the use of theology? Religion, after all, does
not pretend to knowledge. It asks only for faith. Theology in-
tends to be a science. Yet it cannot verify what it offers as knowledge. Lacking this, what utility can it have?

This is the basis for the final rejection of theology. It is made
by devout souls, who rely, as they say, on the heart to bring
them to God. We should attend to what they say. In fact we
should attend particularly when theologians say it, for it is then
better said. In the Christian religion faith does go beyond what
in this world we can know. For one thing, Christianity is concerned with the next world; we simply are not there yet, and no
direct confirmation about it will be possible until we do get
there. But faith can be strengthened and sustained in this world.
It is strengthened and sustained by living in accordance with
that faith. The realization of sin, the practice of asceticism, the
acceptance of the unity of mankind under God, a readiness for
martyrdom, submission to transfiguration, these, says a theologian in one of the papers read to us, are the necessary elements

in the Christian response to God. Another theologian might express these differently, specify a different number. But these varying forms unite in making plain to reason that the return to God starts from our recognition of severance from Him, and requires that our secularism be transformed. We cannot serve Mammon and God. It is true that where man's treasure is, there will his heart be also. These are theological propositions. If their truth is questioned, they cannot be verified by further theological reasoning. Only in action can they be tested and belief in their truth be strengthened. The answer to the charge that, lacking verification, theology has no application is that its verification is found in its application. That is the hardest lesson a theologian has to learn.

Even as I accept this conclusion and recognize how often and how readily I myself try to substitute theological thinking for religious living, there arises also a question. Why can we not get in religion hard, verified knowledge of fact? The kind of thing we get in science. This has been a long essay, and the process of thinking it out and writing it has been longer. Throughout all this length runs one constant theme, the difficulties, the ambiguities, the perplexities we encounter when we try to obtain knowledge of God. The situation is provoking. It is to me, and I imagine this essay has made it so to others. It provokes a question. Why has not God arranged it so that at least knowledge of His existence could be easily obtained, plainly and surely confirmed?

Why not? While thinking on this, frequently with vexation and irritation, it finally did come to me that every difficulty we find in trying to obtain knowledge of God is a difficulty He encounters in making Himself plain to us. If He speaks, it must be in our language, what we understand. If He makes Himself visible, it must be in a form human senses can take in. With respect to every means there is a threshold set by our capacities. We can see the lightning, learn how to produce it, prove our knowledge is knowledge by producing lightning on demand. By what in the Heavens is God's existence to be made certain? By a sign? Every sign requires interpretation, and all interpretations are ambiguous. By His own presence? Not as incarnate in human form. That was tried and gave no proof. The presence must be

God in His own nature, nakedly Himself. And man is to see and know. There is to be no fright, no overwhelming of our present independence and freedom. We are to know beyond the peradventure of a doubt that God is, for we are to see Him face to face, and are to confirm what we see by the test of the second look. We are to do this and live. More, we are to retain our present capacity to ignore Him. We could not. Even if we lived, we should no longer be free. That is the issue, knowledge *versus* human freedom. We cannot have both and be men. But freedom and faith are possible.

The Wisdom of the Greeks

BY HELMUT KUHN

○

I

'God of Abraham, God of Isaac, God of Jacob, not of the philosophers and savants.' Since these words of the *Mémorial* of 1654 were thrown on paper, repeated protests have been raised against the adulteration of our Biblical knowledge of God by an admixture of non-Biblical or non-Christian elements of thought. The source of these alien elements has generally been in philosophy, and philosophy, by and large, meant the intellectual legacy of Greece in contra-distinction to the religious legacy of Judaism. In relating the Bible to non-Christian knowledge of God, we may be allowed to identify the latter with what is somewhat vaguely described as the Hellenic-philosophical ingredient of theology.

The attempts to block the incursions of the 'wisdom of the Greeks' date at least as far back as the fourth century. We remember the scruples felt by the Fathers in admitting into credal formulae non-scriptural terms such as substance, consubstantiality, or hypostasis. And we remember also how these scruples had to be set aside in the interest of a logically coherent statement of doctrine. But the real clash between a Biblical-Pauline conception of God and its Hellenic-humanistic transformation came with the Pelagian controversy and St. Augustine's triumph over the sweet reasonableness of the 'once-born' type of the *homo religiosus*.

From then on the tension between the Hellenic pole and the Biblical pole operates to a considerable extent within the field of ecclesiastic orthodoxy. Moving through a number of phases and interlocking with other antithetical motifs, this tension is noticeable in the struggles of Aristotelianism *versus* Augustinianism, Dominican thought *versus* Franciscan thought, Realism *versus* Nominalism. When the Reformation brought on a fresh outburst of anti-philosophical temper, the protest against Hellenic rationalism in both Calvin and Luther appeared largely as a radicalized restatement of the more radical positions adopted by St. Augustine in the Pelagian controversy. With the doctrines of the total depravity of man and the *servum arbitrium* a philosophical approach to the knowledge of God became a venture of little promise. That the radicalism of the Reformers did not prevent the old dialectic from playing its part in the history of Protestant thought is a well-known fact. The swinging of the pendulum has even been increasing in latitude, and it seems now to have reached so violent an opposition of pole to pole that the antithetical tension threatens to break by excess and so to arrest the dialectical process altogether.

In order to illustrate what is meant by the progressive sharpening and final oversharpening of the antithesis, we distinguish three phases of this process, marked severally by (1) Pascal, (2) Kierkegaard, and (3) the contemporary theology of crisis.

(1) The 'God of the philosophers' whom Pascal rejects is the deistic implication of Descartes' concept of nature. Against this non-Christian idea of God Pascal protests not only in the name of Biblical revelation but also in the name of a concrete philosophy, i.e. a philosophy which, instead of trusting a specious logic, takes into account the facts of real existence. The concrete facts in question are discovered by an analysis of the human situation. In retreating from cosmological philosophy Pascal has a philosophical position to fall back on, and this position, roughly described, is an Augustinian anthropology reconstructed as a rebuttal to Montaigne's neo-pagan anthropology.

It is true, Pascal thinks, that nothing shocks reason so much as the Biblical idea of a living God or the doctrines of man's innate sinfulness and his salvation through Christ's atoning death. But once these Christian teachings are humbly submitted to, the otherwise perplexing facts of man's status exhibit an intelligible pattern. Revelation furnishes the clue to the dialectic of human nature, compacted as it is of misery and grandeur. The knowledge of the heart in whose light this dialectic is grasped does not rule our reason (except the false reason which ministers to the pride of the hateful ego) but it perfects reason's work. The 'heart' for Pascal, far from denoting emotion as contrasted to intelligence, is an organ by which principles are instinctively apprehended.[1]

(2) In Pascal faith retreats from cosmology, the philosophical interpretation of the universe with the terrifying silence of its spaces.[2] Meanwhile philosophy retains a foothold in Christian thought as dialectical anthropology. The retreat is carried one step further by Kierkegaard. The position abandoned here is that of a philosophical anthropology, and, in the place of Descartes' philosophy of nature, Hegel's philosophy of history becomes the target of criticism. And again this criticism purports to free Christian knowledge of God from alien admixtures. Again an edict of expulsion is issued against the 'God of philosophers and savants.' But this time, redefining the relation between Biblical faith and philosophical insight amounts to a divorce. Christianity is no longer conceived as involving a concrete philosophy, but as the paradox confounding philosophy. The discomfiture of reason, Kierkegaard believes, opens our eyes for the Biblical God, our judge and saviour.

The affirmation of a 'divorce,' however, requires qualification. While combatting the Hegelian anthropology with its conception of man as a finite-infinite being evolving through history, Kierkegaard retains a rudimentary anthropology—a speculative theory not, indeed, of human nature, but of a crucial human experience. His idea of crisis faces in two directions. As the defeat of reason it marks a hiatus between philosophy and faith. But the separation is also a link. For this defeat of reason is a self-defeat, induced in a very philosophical manner. In order merely to state the Kierkegaardian conception of crisis we must resort to the dialectic of the finite and infinite or the immanent and transcendent. The approach to an emphatically non-Greek, non-philosophical, Biblical idea of God is thus made by means of an emphatically Greek and philosophical, i.e. Platonic, construction.

(3) The retreat of Biblical faith from philosophy and all its works is complete in the theology of Karl Barth. The verdict on the God of philosophers and savants is of utmost severity, and the word 'divorce' is no longer an overstatement. Again the attitude of the defender of the Biblical knowledge of God reflects the attitude of his adversaries. Pascal, confronted by Cartesianism, tried to bring clear and distinct ideas to bear on a subject matter that evaded the Cartesians. Kierkegaard fought as dialectician against Hegel's then regnant dialectics. Karl Barth, grown up in the climate of Positivism, finds his contemporaries either contemptuous of philosophy or embracing a naturalistic philosophy which, essentially inimical to religion, can be reconciled to Christianity only by a *tour de force;* and he finds theological liberalism committed to precisely this impossible undertaking, the reconciliation of the irreconcilable.

Accordingly Barth does not combat any one philosophy (which can be done only by means of philosophy). Instead he turns his back on philosophy, opposing to the positive sciences of the world a positive dogmatic of the Church. In doing so he liquidates the last bridgehead to which, after the surrender first of cosmology and then of anthropology (or philosophy of history), philosophy was still clinging in Kierkegaard: the idea of crisis as a universal, anthropological concept.

This must seem a surprising statement in view of the fact that Barth's point of view is generally and for very good reasons described as a 'theology of crisis.' Of course, there can be no question of Barth's having actually emancipated himself from Kierkegaard's dialectical-speculative construct of crisis as the occasion for the 'qualitative leap' across the chasm between finitude and the infinite. It may rather be maintained that Barth's central idea, his dialectical view of the understanding of the word of God, is the powerful elaboration of an element in Kierkegaard's thought. However, it must be pointed out that Barth himself is bent on cutting this umbilical cord, reminder of the birth of his thought out of the spirit of philosophy. And this operation is by no means a side issue with him, nor does it result from the idiosyncrasy of a man who happens to dislike philosophy. Barth may be wrong but he must be credited with knowing what he does.

Barth's affirmations on this head leave no room for doubt. In commenting on that crisis which is at the center of his theology, a crisis which does not issue in man's own decision but in 'the divine decision as to whether my act is faith or unbelief, obedience or disobedience, correct or incorrect hearing of the word of God,' he writes: 'It is not one special case among the possibilities of human decision in general. Therefore the understanding of it cannot be framed beforehand in a universal anthropology. Even the most radical of all crises through which man may discover himself in the sense of a general anthropological understanding has nothing to do with this crisis.' [3]

With this warning Barth severs relations not only with Heidegger, whose attempt 'to put philosophy to a theological use' has been discredited by one of his followers,[4] but also with Kierkegaard himself. Barth repudiates the philosophical-Hegelian background of his non-anthropological, non-philosophical concept of crisis. With this declaration of independence from philosophy Barth's theology, in his own opinion, stands and falls. This explains the vehemence with which he rejects Brunner's *Ankneupfungspunkt*. For the 'point of contact' in Brunner's view, while linking human nature to God, is also a link between revelation and philosophy. It is once more the philosophical 'bridgehead' jutting out into the land of Biblical faith.

The uncompromising 'nothing-to-do-with' by means of which Barth tries to force apart the two concepts of human crisis and Christian crisis (the crisis in which the word of God is understood) trails behind it a long series of further 'nothing-to-do-withs.' For the trouble of keeping philosophy at arm's length is unending. There is, for example, the One in philosophy and the one and only God in Christian faith. But the philosophical pursuit of unity, so marked a feature of metaphysics from Parmenides down to contemporary Platonism, achieves, according to Barth, 'absolutely nothing that would have even a distant connection with the knowledge of God.' [5] If the philosopher speaks of God, he means one thing, and if the Christian speaks of God, he means something else, and there is no common ground for the two meanings. For the knowledge of faith 'differs completely from anything else which man calls knowledge, not only in its contents, but in its mode of origin and form as well.' [6]

One can hardly go further in protecting the 'God of Abraham' against a confusion with the 'God of philosophers.' No proof is needed to show that Barth outstrips the anti-rationalism of both Luther and Calvin, and he himself admits to greater consistency on this point of doctrine. But he also claims that he formulates the true principles of the Reformation by conceiving of reformed teaching as the 'absolute' opponent of natural theology.[7] In this view elements of non-Christian or non-Biblical knowledge of God in Christian thought must be regarded as a parasitical growth which ought to be removed as radically and speedily as possible. The opposition which through the ages has kept alive a dialectical interplay reaches at last the point of complete mutual exclusion. The expulsion of the philosopher, the man who deals in Hellenic contraband, from the temple of orthodoxy seems an accomplished fact.

Karl Barth is not alone in working toward the 'great divorce.' No small portion of the energy of modern Protestant thought has been directed toward the same goal. Under the influence of modern anthropology and the study of primitive religion Rudolf Otto has developed his idea of the Numinous.[8] This psycho-theological concept is to Schleiermacher's idea of 'feeling of absolute dependence' as Barth's 'unique' crisis to Kierkegaard's anthropologically universal crisis. In both cases there is a shift from the trans-rational to the irrational. Anders Nygren, finally, has furnished the masterpiece of the art of dissection. The three volumes of his well-known work are devoted to showing that the Greek-Platonic idea of love ($\xi\varrho o\varsigma$) and the New Testament idea of love ($\dot\alpha\gamma\dot\alpha\pi\eta$) have 'nothing to do' with each other and that their admittedly fertile intercourse through eighteen or nineteen centuries of historical Christendom has been an entirely illegitimate affair.[9]

Christian faith is extricated from its entanglements with pagan philosophy by an emphasis on its irrational elements. The same effect is achieved by emphasizing, on the other hand, the rationalistic and, potentially, anti-Christian elements in Hellenic civilization. This has been done by C. N. Cochrane,[10] who defined classical thought in contradistinction to Christian thought as dualistic, revolving upon the dichotomy of form and matter. The tendency at work here is not new, and crisis theology merely carries a step further an endeavor pursued before by liberalism. Liberal historical theology, imbued as it was in frequent cases with the spirit of contemporary nationalism, adopted tacitly or explicitly the Principle of Nationality according to which the culture of every people is informed by a unique and immutable entelechy, and national history is to be understood as the unfolding of this innate form. It is, then, a foregone conclusion that an association of Hebrew ideas with Greek ideas can form only an inorganic compound of heterogeneous elements. In the spirit of this philosophy Adolf von Harnack in his classic work viewed the development of Christian doctrine as a progressive adulteration of Christian faith with elements of Hellenic philosophy.

Probing for vulnerable tissues, the instruments of theological surgery advance with converging incisions into the body of tradition. The objective, to be sure, is not analysis but affirmation, with Karl Barth and his followers even a prophetic affirmation. The debt of gratitude we owe to Barth is perhaps not overstated in saying that, for large areas of the Protestant world, he rediscovered Christianity. But the analytic surgery which goes with that affirmative move (every move in human thought is a counter move) is terrifying. It is particularly alarming that historical study should confound history. Yet such seems to be the conclusion arrived at.

As a witness for the historical liquidation of history we may hear a British theologian. Dean W. R. Matthews,[11] surveying the attempt to frame a speculative doctrine of God—an attempt that extends 'over all Christian centuries, up to and including the seventeenth'—deems it 'one of the most impressive monuments of the human intellect' but, at the same time, a failure. The construction turned out to be 'inadequate to the Christian experience of God and even, in fact, issued in a contradiction of that experience.' The blame for this failure lies not with the theologians but with their intellectual tools. 'Philosophy, as they were acquainted with it, was incapable of fulfilling the task which they imposed upon it. Created in a milieu which was not Christian, it remained in some measure alien to the Christian view of the world.'

It appears that the divorce of faith from philosophy involves the divorce of contemporary Christianity from, according to Dean Matthews' computation, seventeen centuries of the Christian past. There seems excuse for those who feel some alarm at this prospect.

II

In speaking of Barth I have made reference to theology's 'declaration of independence.' It is difficult not to look upon the proclaimed autonomy as a patent illusion. To take it at its face value one would have to shut one's eyes to the fact that Barth, with all his anti-philosophical bias, rides the wave of a powerful philosophical movement. Viewed in a larger perspective, dialectical theology appears as one of the numerous manifestations of modern irrationalism. The weapons with which Barth combats the intruder philosophy are borrowed from the armory of philosophy.

In the progressive alienation of theology from philosophy, it is not only theology that moves away from philosophy. Philosophy also is on the move, and it moves in a direction which makes it increasingly difficult for theology to maintain the ancient alliance. This movement of philosophy may be roughly described as leading from idealism toward naturalistic pragmatism, and in its general tendency it is a movement away from the classic, i.e. Platonic-Aristotelian, tradition. So the defection of theology from its alliance with philosophy goes hand in hand with a defection of philosophy from its loyalty to the Hellenic origin of metaphysics. The philosophy that receives an order of eviction at the hands of the theologians of Barth's school is no longer the 'wisdom of the Greeks' but a wisdom of more recent date.

Remembering the three stages of the process of alienation as represented severally by Pascal, Kierkegaard, and Barth, we find each one of the three defenders of faith under a very natural illusion. They all tend to identify the contemporary philosophical doctrine which they combat with 'the philosophy,' typifying the work of human reason. The philosopher whose conception of God Pascal decries as un-Christian is the Cartesian philosopher. Similarly Kierkegaard, while pouring scorn upon Hegel, seems in no doubt that Hegel's reason is Reason as such. Barth does not escape this illusion either. It is even a cruder and more destructive illusion with him than with his predecessors, because he happens to live in a time of the disintegration of philosophy. In mistaking an ill-fitting modern disguise of reason for reason's true form, it was only too easy for him to dismiss philosophy as an unprofitable servant or worse, a fiendish counselor.

In discussing the hiddenness of God, Barth portrays rational knowledge as characterized by the following three features: (1) it limits its object; (2) it brings its object under control; (3) it attests a basic oneness of knower and the object of knowledge.[12]

In contradistinction to this rational knowledge as a human achievement Barth defines the only authentic knowledge of God as non-rational knowledge, imparted through grace under the form of the Word of God. (1) The true God, so the counter-portrayal of scriptural knowledge shows, can in no way be encompassed by us, not even dialectically as the 'unlimited' or 'infinite' which is still a subtle attempt to enclose Him within our (human) system. (2) Far from being at our disposal the authentic knowledge of God is given us, and we have not even so much freedom as either to receive or to reject the gift. The door can be opened from the inside only. (3) Rather than being one with God we have no one feature resembling God, and the scriptural idea of a man as the image of God means merely that we are called upon by God to bear witness in our existence to His existence.

So we have two types of knowledge, neatly adjusted to each other by way of contrast. When a so-defined rational knowledge presumes, under the name of natural theology, to rise to God, using vestiges of God in the created world as stepping stones, it undertakes the impossible. For God it substitutes a human fiction, an idol, "ushering a foreign God into the precincts of the church.' So traditional Catholic and much of Protestant theology owes its existence to an attempt 'to unite Yahweh with Baal, the triune God of holy scripture with the ontology of Aristotelian and Stoic philosophy.' [13] It is true that this same traditional theology tries to safeguard both its human sanity and Christian humility by consistently maintaining the essential incomprehensibility and undefinability of God. But even the claim to obtain elements of a non-scriptural knowledge of God through God's 'general revelation' and by means of analogy ('*analogia entis* is the invention of Antichrist'),[14] betrays a 'pagan component' in the concept of God.

The preceding argument turns upon a characterization of rational knowledge of no uncertain origin. Barth's concept of reason belongs in the lineage of post-Kantian idealism, modified under the influence of both Nietzsche's philosophy of the Will to Power and modern pragmatism. It is reason as conceived by an epistemology which has for its metaphysical premise the self-deification of man. It is not reason as such but reason as some people in the era of incipient and finally full-fledged irrationalism have come to think of it.

Viewed in the light of a less metaphysically biased inspection, rational knowledge shows none of the traits ascribed to it by Barth in unison with an idealistic-pragmatic epistemology. So, in opposition to Barth's triad, the following antitheses may recommend themselves. (1) To know a thing does not mean to limit it. In point of fact, the object of knowledge, however exhaustively it is known, persists in indefeasible transcendence outside the sphere of knowledge. (2) Knowledge, far from being control or mastery (*mächtig sein*) over its object, is won only through self-abdication and submission under the nature of the object. And this basic subordination is the price we pay for whatever measure of control we are able to win over objects. (3) While rational knowledge may require a degree of likeness between knower and object, its meaning is misconstrued by the idealistic conception of an ultimate unity of the two. We are not evil in knowing evil, nor good in knowing the good.

A critic might contest this 'realistic' interpretation of knowledge and side with Hegel, Nietzsche, and Barth. But he surely must admit that that rational knowledge which Barth banishes from theology has 'nothing to do with' Plato's and Aristotle's conception of rational knowledge and reason. Their thinking was dominated by what Goethe called *Seinsfrömmigkeit*. They approached reality with reverential awe as spectators of a more-than-human spectacle. For them knowing was a kind of non-bodily seeing, and they thought of the operational aspect of knowledge as an unveiling of that which is. Only a daring sophist, Protagoras, seems to have suggested a pragmatic interpretation of knowledge by equating truth with expediency. But the ontology which, thanks to Plato and Aristotle, ruled supreme in Occidental metaphysics and theology had for its moral prerequisite the devout and, in its advanced stages, rapturous acceptance of that which exists independent of our pleasure or approval. Only at a relatively recent date, knowledge came to be interpreted, or misinterpreted, as domination. The heathen idol which Barth overthrows does not bear the features of a Greek god. He merely brushes a modern gimcrack from the mantlepiece.

The student of *Die Kirchliche Dogmatik* can hardly help feeling that the dichotomy by which rational knowledge, autonomous and incurably pagan, is cut off from the Biblical knowledge of the Church is brought about by an act of violence. What the Latin poet [15] says about nature applies also to reason in theology: driven out with the pitchfork she at once slips back into the house. Barth's *Dogmatics* is rather less of a running commentary to Holy Scripture than most of theology, ancient or modern; and he is more willing to bend the text to the dictates of his doctrinal system than most of his contemporary fellow-theologians. The above-quoted example of the image of God, interpreted by Barth as an image that bears no resemblance to the original, shows in how lordly a manner he deals with the Bible wherever it does not seem sufficiently Biblical. The humble and self-effacing service at the Word, the virtue of historical theology at its best, is foreign to Barth's neo-orthodoxy.

It is not our purpose to trip up the great man and to point out, with ungenerous satisfaction, how even he slips occasionally from the narrow and arduous path of strictly Biblical-exegetic

argument. No petty inconsistencies are at issue. We rather believe we discover in the pages of his monumental work the
nemesis of reason in the grand manner. Reason, refused admission through the main portal and sneaking in through the back
door, is no less imperious for being less honored. On the contrary, we find lodged in the very core of Barth's *Dogmatics* a
rather uninhibited rationalism, reminiscent of the more hazard-
ous *Logos* speculations of Christian Neo-Platonists.

Taking the concept of the Holy Trinity as a test, we com-
pare Barth's treatment with a recent essay on the same topic by
Leonard Hodgson.[16] The two interpretations have more than
one feature in common, as, for instance, the care with which
they avoid heresies such as modalism or, a more difficult task,
subordinationism. Both, of course, admit that the idea of Trinity is a theologoumenon not found in the Bible but arrived at
through an exegesis of Scripture by the early Church. But here
the characteristic and, at the same time, rather paradoxical di-
vergence begins. Hodgson, the Anglican, a believer in general
revelation and the metaphysical-theological competence of
reason, begins with carefully sifting the Biblical evidence. Not
so Barth. He, the despiser of reason (rational knowledge has
'nothing to do with' knowledge imparted through the Word),
applies himself at once to framing a dialectic-speculative construction. 'God reveals himself,' or 'I show myself.' The triadic
structure of all self-revelation as expressed in these sentences
rather than some particular truth imparted by the Christian
revelation is the root from which, according to Barth, the trini-
tarian dogma grows. 'Any child knows,' he writes, that this
exegetic dogma 'operates with certain philosophical terms of the
outgoing pagan antiquity.' [17] (Dean Matthews' problem of the
'intellectual tools!') Nonetheless, he continues, 'its statements
admit of being regarded as, not directly but indirectly, identical
with those of the Biblical witness to revelation.' The idea of an
indirect identity bears a distressing family-likeness to the afore-
mentioned idea of an image that does not resemble its model.

By repudiating Greek philosophy and yet, constrained by the
tradition of the Western World, drawing heavily upon it, Barth
creates a disturbing intellectual twilight, which also plays around

his idea of God as one. Naturally he dwells upon the difference between the ontological concept of God, the *summum ens,*
with its Aristotelian antecedents on the one hand, and the God
who reveals Himself through work and action (*Werk und
Handeln*),[18] the God of Abraham, Isaac, and Jacob, the creator,
judge, and saviour, on the other. And he widens this difference into incompatibility by leaving out of account the fact
that the ontologically conceived God of Aristotle and after him
of the Christian Aristotelians is life and actuality ('being-at-
work'). This omission enables him to define once more his
method by means of an antithesis. To the metaphysical principle
operari sequitur esse he opposes his *esse sequitur operari.*[19] Thus
he seems to circumscribe his position with a clear though somewhat harshly drawn outline. But the twilight that blurs all con-
tours is still upon us. For we remember that the discussion in the
course of which these affirmations are made is based upon the
idea that our knowledge of God has for its 'real and primary essence' God's self-knowledge.[20] And we also remember that the
concept of divine life as self-knowledge [21] is as certainly in Aristotle as it is absent in the Bible. It may still be the acceptable
result of permissible exegesis. But is it permissible to Barth?

All these observations urge upon us an important conclusion
first relating to the place of Barth's theology in contemporary
Christian thought, and, in the second place, pointing in the direction of true progress.

As Paul Tillich [22] has once pointed out with reference to a
cultural-sociological context, and as Reinhold Niebuhr's theology throughout implies, Protestant thought has reached a critical point. The Protestant *ethos,* directed as it is against anything that in Christian teaching and practice might obscure the
principle of justification through grace alone (the principle of
Christian individualism), has been eclipsed in our time. As a
negative or critical principle, this Protestant *ethos* requires an
antithesis within Christianity. At the present moment, however,
the dialectical tension has spent itself, and the protest to be made
is no longer the phase of a dialectic indigenous to Christianity.
For the challenge comes now from outside, from a secularism
that denies Christianity along with its intellectual-metaphysical

implications, reducing to mere fictions the key terms of the language of both metaphysics and religion, such as God, soul, eternal life, and the like. The challenge is none the less an extraneous one for frequently disguising its nature with the trappings of liberal theology. And it is a challenge of fatal decisiveness, because it confronts us to an ever-increasing degree with a secularism of fanatical belief rather than of skepticism. It summons to battle demonic powers that are anti-Christian as well as anti-rational.

Through Karl Barth's *Römerbrief* a generation of Protestant theologians was reminded of the primal truths of Christianity. For many he rediscovered the meaning of the words 'sin' and 'salvation.' The force of his elemental reaffirmation accounts for the powerful response. The battle he won was a victory over non-Christian or anti-Christian secularism and, by the same taken, a victory of ecumenical Protestantism. But, we venture to suggest, he tragically misconstrues the meaning of his deed by placing upon it the interpretation of an artificially radicalized, fanatically anti-philosophical and anti-humanistic super-Protestantism. Artificial is the position because its counterposition, the target of controversy in the *Church Dogmatics,* is not identical with the real antagonist. Barth's fulminations against the Romish Baal and his Hellenic ancestry are out of date. How sadly the true picture is distorted becomes clear when Barth interprets the fight of the Confessional Church against Hitler's totalitarian state (that venomous outgrowth of a secular irrationalism) as a phase in the Protestant struggle against natural theology.[23] *Hannibal ante portas!* But the factions in the beleaguered city continue to quarrel.

If these conclusions hold, they have an important bearing upon our problem, the relation in which the Hellenic-philosophical elements of Christian thought stand to Biblical faith. In fact, they point toward a possible solution. Once we admit that the essence of Christian faith is not to be established by a purge (anti-philosophical and anti-Hellenic criticism being the purgative), we prepare ourselves for a change of mind on two basic issues.

First, we cease to look upon reason as a source of theological insight with a sense of grudging distrust as though it were our first duty as Christians to keep it from overstepping its bounds. This is a duty too, but it is a greater duty not to blindfold our love to God by severing it from our love of knowledge. The fear of error, here as elsewhere, should not be allowed to overwhelm our desire for truth. Truth is indivisible. If Christianity is true at all, it must be the truth about ourselves and the world we live in. And then there can be nothing in this world, either in nature or in society, which does not in some measure bear witness to this truth. Strictly speaking, there can be no non-Christian sources of knowledge. Faith (*fides quaerens intellectum* rather than *fides fugiens intellectum*) finds truth not only in the mouths of babes but in the mouths of heathen as well.

No new critical statement is required, no new protest against the authority of reason or of ecclesiastic institutions, but a constructive affirmation. And this affirmation cannot dispense with reason as the constructive faculty of the mind. This brings us to the second issue involved.

It will be necessary to make clear what we mean by reason. If we acquiesce in current interpretations of reason as an expression of will to power, or as a sublimation of libido, or as an organic response to environmental stimuli, or as a tool for social and generally vital adjustment, our task becomes hopeless. In using these concepts—and many do so unwittingly—we are committed to a metaphysics that is as adverse to Christianity as it generally is to any 'spiritual,' i.e. non-materialistic and non-naturalistic, interpretation of life. Inadvertently we have then become partners to the divorce of reason from faith, and our attempts at reconciliation will come under the condemnation of 'appeasement policy.'

In order to escape this danger we may have to reverse the direction of the theology of crisis to the extent that it is heading toward irrationalism. Instead of taking part in browbeating the intellect, the sport widely engaged in by modern intellectuals in all camps, Fascist, Communist, and Christian, we might try to restore reason to its real status, and thereby make it again eligible for an alliance with faith. Instead of indulging in an absurd fear of the 'wisdom of the Greeks' (absurd in those who lend a willing ear to all kinds of modern sophistry), we may try a road to the truth of the Gospel which brings us into closer vicinity to Athens than the highway of modernity does.

III

The Bible as the document of God's dealings with His chosen people and of the earthly life, teaching, suffering, and resurrection of our Lord Jesus Christ is the revealed basis of our faith. Only by accepting this principle of scriptural revelation are we Christians in conformity with the meaning which past centuries have conferred upon that name and which we are not free to change. Here we take this principle for granted and therefore leave out of account the point of view, sometimes called liberal but actually non-Christian, according to which special revelation can teach us only that which is, or can be, known through general revelation. In adopting this latter view we should be free to place Plato, Aristotle, and modern science on the same footing with the Bible. But in order to simplify my argument I do not wish even to consider this possibility.

In the process of appropriating revealed truth we try to think it, and so build up a theology. But evidently the materials furnished by the Bible are not sufficient for constructing a theology. For whereas theology is essentially systematic, the Bible is essentially historical. In rearing its doctrinal edifice, theology needs systematic-constructive, non-Biblical concepts. To obtain these concepts theology must apply to philosophy, thereby contracting a debt to the Greeks. A great but unavoidable risk is involved in this debtorship.

Putting the matter more simply, we may assert that theology, whatever its specific definition, assuredly must be a theory. But theory is by origin and character a Hellenic venture, and whoever engages in theory follows the Greeks. While an indirect contact, through the Bible, with the Hellenic world is inescapable, we can be good Christians without being directly touched by the Greek genius. But as Christian theologians we must Hellenize, and there is no remedy to that.

Of course, there had been high wisdom and profound thinking long before the Greeks set to work, especially in China and India. But it was the Greeks who contributed the strict concept and practice of *theoria* along with its correlate, the idea of objectivity. Addressing themselves to the infinite but orderly multiplicity of objects with the reiterated question: 'What is this?'—they sought an answer expressible not merely in words but in terms, i.e. in words that are made to denote in varying contexts an identical and definable meaning. To this Hellenic *theoria* we owe our astronomy and physics, our airplanes and atomic bombs. Applied to reality as a whole rather than to one of its limited aspects, *theoria* engenders philosophy. 'Christ came into the world to save sinners.' It is possible to understand the meaning of this affirmation and to accept it as true without having any dealings with Greek science. But as soon as, dissatisfied with an elementary understanding, we ask: 'What is sin?,' 'What is man?,' 'What is salvation?,' in other words, as soon as we become theologians, we take in hand a business of which the evangelists and apostles knew nothing, but which we have learned from the Greeks. In addition, we ask questions some of which are identical not only in form but also in content with philosophical questions.

Christian theology is *theoria* placed in the service of Christianity. In employing this foreign-born servant, Christianity incurs a risk, because, in order to become theologically fruitful, *theoria* must (a) be something more than a mere formal method, and again it must (b) under no circumstances be allowed to become so much more than a method that it turns into the vehicle of pagan religion. While the latter contention (b) is self-evident, the former (a) is not amenable to proof in the present context. With a view to making it plausible we may point out that the sphere within which theology moves is that of *theoria* in the more radical sense, i.e. theory as directed toward total reality rather than one of its aspects. Because of its intrinsically speculative character the endeavor of theology has become historically continuous not only with Greek science in general but especially with that more emphatically Greek enterprise which Aristotle called sometimes 'first philosophy' and sometimes theology. And it is, to say the least, improbable that Christian theology should be able to break away from this adopted ancestry without destroying itself.

This surplus over and above mere formal method which theology receives from the Greeks as an implication of *theoria* may be described as affirmative ontology. It involves the following principles: (a) reality is a meaningful whole existing independently of our knowledge of it—the principle of classical realism; (b) man is endowed with a faculty for understanding, however dimly, the meaning of reality—the principle of classical rationalism; (c) being and goodness ('value') belong together; by discovering that which is, man becomes apprised of what he should do —the principle of classical pragmatism. These three principles, basic to philosophy from Plato on, are summed up in the assertion: 'man finds himself living in a cosmos.'

Whenever this affirmative ontology as the basis of a rational faith is destroyed, *theoria* ceases to be applicable to total reality and, by the same token, the language of theology is robbed of its meaning. Theological thinking, so weakened at its core, may then lose its foothold in the territory which is held in common by both Judaic tradition and Greek philosophers: the belief that the world is real as well as essentially good, the evil in it stemming from human failure rather than from cosmic necessity. As this conviction is shaken, the path lies open to errors which are repugnant to Jew and Greek alike. The reality of the world is called in question by idealistic philosophies which de-substantialize the cosmos into the veil of appearance, thus entering in conjunction with Hindoo thought. Or the goodness of the world is denied along with its rationality as in the secular type of existential philosophy, which seems to lean toward a Persian conception of existence. Reading Martin Heidegger's analysis of man's status as a being-thrown-into-existence, or Jean-Paul Sartre's description of the fundamental experience of nausea, we find it difficult not to associate these views with the Gnostic idea of a world which, framed by evil demons, keeps the soul enthralled within the multitudinous prison walls of body, sublunar world, and celestial spheres.[24] When Plotinus wrote his anti-Gnostic pamphlet on the excellence of the cosmos against its detractors,[25] he joined a battle in which philosophers fought as allies of Christian theologians. The same will be true of any modern philosophical vindication of the fundamental thesis: 'man finds himself living in a cosmos.'

If there is danger in surrendering the idea of cosmos as the objective correlate of affirmative ontology, there is danger also in accepting this idea in its unqualified Greek form as denoting an ultimate, self-sufficient reality. 'We worship God rather than heaven and earth,' St. Augustine states pointedly.[26] To become assimilable by Christian thought the ancient cosmos must suffer its degradation (or allow for its exaltation) to the status of a creation. The ultimate must become the penultimate. It may well refuse to submit to this transfiguration. Whenever this refusal occurs, philosophy becomes the advocate of paganism by divinizing the cosmos. The Platonists of the School of Chartres identifying the *anima mundi* in the *Timaeus* with the Holy Ghost, the Averroists denying as strict Aristotelians the idea of creation and the immortality of the individual soul, Emerson interpreting Christ as one of the prophets of the Over-Soul—these are a few examples of the rebellious longevity of paganism in the medium of speculative thought. The 'god of the philosophers' may indeed turn out to be a member of the Olympic family or a modern likeness of the lord Dionysus. The fear of philosophical paganism is not absurd in itself. But we maintain that the fear is untimely. The Greek heaven does not stir to life in this somber century of ours. What we have to contend with today are the demons of the lower regions, pagan in the sense of pre-Hellenic and pre-rational heathenism, and hailing from no one country in particular.

IV

Reflecting upon the relation in which theological exegesis stands to the text of the Bible we may enunciate the following principle: exegesis is successful to the extent that it combines intellectual coherence and penetration with fidelity to scriptural revelation. And this fidelity is to be gauged not in terms of a point-for-point correspondence but as an adequacy of balanced meaning. Implied in this principle is a more narrowly defined criterion of easier applicability. Systematic exegesis as a human construct must crystallize round a central idea or key concept, and this key concept must be so chosen as to possess both a maximum of construction potentialities and centrality in the Bible; and the latter requirement may involve centrality also in the teachings of Jesus. Thus the key concept will face in two directions: toward reason and toward revelation, corresponding to its two main virtues, constructiveness and fidelity. Its constructiveness will show its dependence upon philosophy and, therewith, a tradition of Greek rather than Jewish-Christian origin.

In Reinhold Niebuhr's theology, which I may here use in illustration of my point, the key concept is the idea of the dual nature of man as a historical being: immersed in history and, at the same time, transcending history. This concept has a fidelity in so far as it is rooted in Christ's teaching of the Kingdom of God; and it owes its systematic constructiveness to its Hegelian background. In the case of Barth's theology the diagnosis reads as follows: The key concept is the understanding of God's Word in the situation of crisis. Its constructiveness is derived directly from Kierkegaard's existential dialectic, indirectly from Hegel. Its fidelity consists in expressing the Biblical teaching of man's obedience toward God. This Biblical foundation is of doubtful adequacy. The emphasis is on the Old Testament *ethos,* 'Thy servant hears . . .,' rather than on the specific message of Christ. the linguistic clue to Barth's dogmatics is the close etymological kinship which links *hören* (hear) to *Gehorsam* (obedience). So dominant is the idea of obedience with Barth that man's love to God is understood by him as the condition of 'being permitted to love God' (*lieben dürfen*).[27]

Barth is neither the first nor the only Christian theologian at whose hands the love to God as preached by Christ suffers diminution. We rather observe that the process of gradual estrangement and final divorce of philosophy from theology as sketchily indicated in the first part of this paper is bound up with a removal of charity, especially its human aspect, from the center of theological thinking. This is the more curious because the Hegelian dialectic which, transformed but still identifiable, tends to replace charity, is itself a speculative transformation of that Christian concept. The dialectic of the Spirit, as Hegel's early writings show, was originally conceived as the dialectic of Christian love.

In this connection we recall once more the three stages of the progress toward irrationalism and their several representatives. Although in Pascal's 'acosmic' thought love is no longer visible as the power 'that moves the sun and the other stars,' it still holds undiminished sway over the human heart. In pages that have been called the finest in all French literature he places the order of charity (which is the order of Christ, of wisdom, and saintliness) as high above the order of spirit (the order of Archimedes) as spirit in its turn is above body. For Pascal, true follower of St. Augustine and St. Bernard of Clairvaux, charity is 'the sole object of Scripture,' everything else in it being mere figure.

As we come to Kierkegaard, we find the dominion over the mind transferred to a power called 'passion'—the aspiration through which the existing individual relates himself to the Infinite. This passion may, through a miraculous transformation, become the 'happy passion' which is love. But the social dimension of this love suffers atrophy in the fierce individualism of the philosophy of crisis. It is curious to reflect that the omnibus,[28] the one among Pascal's numerous inventions which is directly traceable to his idea of charity, must have been the vehicle of abomination to Kierkegaard.

At the third stage, in Karl Barth, charity, especially as love to God and love of the neighbor, is at several removes from the constructive center. The ethics incorporated in his *Dogmatics* is as pure an example of a *Gehorsamsethik* (ethics of obedience) as Kant's doctrine of the Categorical Imperative. In the definition of love, the propelling force, the 'panting after God' of the Psalms, is omitted and the static element, the *adhaerere Deo*, alone is retained, sharpened by the existentialist idea of the absolute risk involved in this surrender. To love, Barth defines with a characteristically negative formula, is 'to will not to be oneself or to have oneself without the beloved object.' [29]

But what becomes of charity if the surgeon's knife is plied with the determination to extirpate relentlessly all Greek accretions may be seen from Anders Nygren's well-known book. After the analyst has put love through his de-Hellenization procedure, he

feels emboldened to write (cold-bloodedly, in a table that offers
a neatly symmetrical conspectus) that the term 'love' as denoting
'man's love to God' is used in Christianity 'with reservations.' [30]
Here we have the quintessence of the nothing-to-do-with radicalism which, by means of nuclear fission, explodes a tradition of
some seventeen-hundred years' standing. The insistence on having nothing in Christianity but things of Christian origin makes
of Christianity a less than Christian thing.

Instead of proceeding in this centrifugal direction, one might
try to start again from the point where the wrong turn was
taken. By placing once more love in the germinant center of
theology (the real *agape,* neither speculatively transfigured by
Hegel, nor maimed by Professor Nygren's Procrustean practices),
we might find ourselves in a position to take full advantage of
Greek philosophy without falling a prey to the paganism in it.

Some sketchy remarks may be sufficient to show whither the
execution of this program would take us.

The idea of love as dawning in the prophetic literature, the
Psalms, and the wisdom literature and shining in full clarity in
the New Testament covers three distinct aspects of a unified
reality. It is (1) love of God to man, (2) love of man to God, and
(3) love of man to man. In one sense, the first and the third aspects belong together. In the two cases in which the object of
love is man, love is, so to speak, the inner shaft within a wider
but less intensely luminous stream of light. The outer court sur-
rounding the core (the love of man) is the love of 'heaven and
earth,' i.e. of the created universe. No such concomitant can be
associated with man's love to God, for it encompasses all differ-
entiations. Created things are loved aright only if they are loved
'in God.' In another sense, the second and the third aspects belong together. Resorting to a familiar and unavoidable imagery,
we may describe God's love to his creature as descending love,
whereas man's love to God and its expansion into man's love of
his fellowmen is ascending love.

According to Anders Nygren the ascending love is *eros* and
belongs in Hellenic antiquity, whereas Christian *agape* is descending love; and the two, he holds, are quite incompatible
with each other. To maintain his thesis the Swedish theologian

must virtually cancel the second aspect of love and disparage the first and greatest commandment. He must further contend that the love of man to man, like God's love to man, is a descending and 'uncaused' love, the love of sinners, and among them of a particularly odious class, the 'publicans,' the ancient Jewish equivalent to the modern 'collaborationist.'

Eros, for Plato, is the desire 'to beget in beauty,' in other words, it is a creative principle directed toward perfection. As such it is an ascending movement, aiming at an assimilation of man to God, at a self-perfection which involves passionate concern, even to the point of martyrdom, for the perfection of his fellows. All this fits very well into Nygren's dichotomic scheme. But the other side of the picture does not so fit and is, accordingly, overlooked. The fact is disregarded that the Godward ascent of the Platonic *eros* presupposes throughout a descending move of divine initiative. To call the demiurge, the 'father of all things' in the *Timaeus,*[31] 'ungrudging' may seem a very frigid declaration of divine love. Likewise the concern for man which is ascribed to divine nature in the tenth book of the *Laws* may be discounted as having only an obscure relation to Plato's general ontology. But the decisive argument taken from Plato's cosmology is incontrovertible. In the *Timaeus* the universe is interpreted as a living whole, wonderfully designed for one purpose only: by manifesting order it shows man how to make his life orderly and so to approach God. There is no ascent without a staircase contrived for this purpose and built, so to speak, from above downward. Although Plato is very reticent on the descending move, he says enough to show that he is aware of its indispensability. The circuit of love (the Heraclitean oneness of the upward road and the road downward) determines the rhythm of his living universe.

To state this is not to make a Christian out of Plato. The chasm that separates Platonic *eros* from Christian *agape* remains wide. But we are now in a position to define the difference in terms that preserve the element of identity. In Plato the emphasis is on the human pole of the circuit and, accordingly, on the upward or Godward struggle of the soul. In the New Testament all the emphasis is on the opposite pole, on God and the descending power of His creative love. The rise under the propulsion of *eros* is chiefly human endeavor and achievement, while the rise of the soul aflame with charity is essentially passive, the suffering of God's uplifting grace. But neither is passivity lacking in the Platonic ascent (the Platonic *mania* prefigures Christian grace), nor is strenuous endeavor absent from the upward surge of *agape*. 'Be ye perfect,' Christ commands.[32] And St. Paul, using the very Greek metaphor of the Isthmian games, compares eternal life with the laurel wreath that crowns the victorious athlete. 'So run, that ye may obtain,' he admonishes.[33]

In his attempt to prove that *agape* is the 'direct opposite' of *eros* [34] Nygren defines *agape,* the love of God toward his creatures, as spontaneous or 'uncaused,' i.e. not called forth by any excellence in the object. On Platonic principles there must be some want in the lover which prompts him to desire a perfection not yet his own. Evidently such cannot be the love that God bears to us. Hence, Nygren argues, this divine love, the *agape* of which love of the neighbor is a human reflex, must be 'the direct opposite' of *eros,* and the two must have 'nothing to do with each other.'

For one who argues with less heat the facts may speak a different language. Love, ascending or descending, creates perfection. This is its very essence. This is, at the same time, the bond that links *agape* to *eros* as it also links God's descending love to our aspiring one. Holding fast to this idea as to the essential meaning of love, we may then distinguish two different manifestations of this essentially unitary love. On the human level, love, called forth by perfection, creates new perfection (*amor ectypus*). In God, as *amor originarius,* it creates gratuitously unprecedented perfection. The question why God created the world cannot be asked without blasphemy, because the doubt it expresses springs from the denial of the perfection of God's creation. But in a sense, an answer to this prohibited question may be supplied by an affirmation familiar to Christian theology from its inception on. The creation, it is affirmed, and especially man owe their existence to the sheer bounty of God. They exist for God in the sense that they manifest His glory. And this, incidentally, is also Plato's view (in the *Laws*) [35] of the relation between man and divinity. Rightly understood, this affirmation denotes a way of life rather than a hypothesis concerning the origin of the world.

By calling God's love 'uncaused' in the sense in which Nygren takes this term we bring it dangerously close to what is humanly called 'whim.' 'Called forth by a cause never fully to be understood by us' would be a more adequate formula, because it protects us against an error to which theology in the age of irrationalism is naturally prone. This error consists in confusing the superrational with the irrational.

If Nygren is right and God's love is 'uncaused,' the same quality must be attributable to the human counterpart or reflex of this love, the love of one's neighbor which the other commandment (second in order but like unto the greatest commandment in dignity) enjoins. It follows that charity among men is in no sense based upon the worth of the object (and, on this occasion, the idea of the infinite value of the human soul is jettisoned as another piece of paganism). This uncaused charity, then, seeks not the good and the worthy but the sinners, publicans, whores, crooks, the scum and the dregs of human society. In corroboration, the parables of the prodigal son and the laborers in the vineyard are invoked and interpreted.

The logic of this argument is questionable. If the rays of charity would actually, like sunshine and rain, fall on the just and the unjust alike, no preference should be given to the wicked. Disregard of the order of righteousness is one thing, its inversion another thing. But graver errors than this one are involved in the idea of an 'uncaused love.' Surely, love among men should be creative of a perfection (in both the lover and the loved one) which is pleasing in the sight of God. Love must, therefore, be animated by the conviction that my brother is not only worth being cared for but that there is nothing in this world which, by its intrinsic worth, makes so ineluctable a demand on my concern for its well-being as my fellowman does. Love does as the good Samaritan did. But even while the lover of man tends the wounds of his fellowman, he ministers to the body as to a tabernacle in which a more precious thing, God's own image, is enshrined. Love wills the perfection of the loved one. In this consists the austerity of love which Socrates and Plato proclaimed as the nature of *eros*. Christian love is greater than *eros* because to this austerity it adds compassionate tenderness, the human reflex of the inscrutability and superabundance of God's love for us. It is a love that has Christ for its prototype in a twofold sense: as Christ crucified He is the perfect lover, and as the living Christ He is the perfect object of love. But in discarding from this love austerity in order to retain only the fierce tenderness of 'uncaused,' i.e. irrational, love, we do not adopt a more Christian view but we sink below the pagan philosophers.

Three motifs are interwoven in the teachings and parables of Christ which illustrate the operation of *agape*. Each of these motifs, rightly understood, helps define the frame of reference within which love must be interpreted. But each may also tempt into a misinterpretation which seems to warrant the 'great divorce' of Hellenic reason from Christian faith.

There is first the sinfulness of man which calls for God's saving grace and forgiveness. Misunderstood as in the dogma of total depravity it destroys the 'circuit of love' by cancelling the ascent with its implications of human initiative. In the second place, since self-righteousness, the chief temptation of social success, can less easily be melted down in the fire of repentance than other forms of sin, Christian love, though addressing itself to all men, shows partiality for the outcast, the underprivileged, and the social failure. Misunderstood, this feature tempts into perverting the circuit of love: the ascending urge of love is transformed into the downward nostalgia of sentimentalism or romanticism. Thirdly, the emphasis on sin and the crisis of repentance and conversion brings the fact of suffering close to the center of the Christian scheme of thought, thereby throwing into bold relief the spiritual significance of physical pain as caused by poverty, illness, hunger, thirst, and cold. Thus the compassionate alleviation of such pain appears as the clearest manifestation of love on the human level. Again this idea lends itself to a misconstruction which deflects the circuit of love so that 'feed the hungry, clothe the naked' appears the sum total of Christian wisdom, and the message of the Kingdom of God is reduced to a social gospel.

The circuit of love is closed in the consummation of love. The Biblical-theological term denoting this consummation is the 'vision of God,' vouchsafed by the sixth of the beatitudes to the 'pure in heart.' Wherever its anti-philosophical and anti-mystical bias tempts theology into minimizing the idea of 'seeing God,' the constructive power of the concept of love is in danger of succumbing to the grand assault of contemporary irrationalism. To the irrationalist deviation we oppose the affirmation of Christian rationalism by an early theologian—an affirmation that in its dual structure admirably expresses the downward path and the upward path of love, its descent into creation, and man's return to God: *gloria enim Dei vivens homo; vita autem hominis visio Dei* (Irenaeus).[36]

NOTES

1. *Pensées,* ed. Léon Brunschvicg, Paris, 1904, no. 282 (II, 203-5).
2. Ibid. no. 206 (II, 127).
3. *Die Lehre vom Worte Gottes. Prolegomena zur Kirchlichen Dogmatik (Die Kirchliche Dogmatik,* vol. I), Munich, 1931, p. 166. Cf. *The Doctrine of the Word of God,* tr. by G. T. Thomson, Edinburgh, 1936, pp. 182 sqq. I have followed Thomson's translation only in part.
4. *Die Lehre vom Worte Gottes,* p. 251. Thomson has misunderstood this passage, rendering *verwerten* with 'evaluate.' The follower referred to is H. E. Eisenhuth, *Der Begriff des Irrationalen als philosophisches Problem,* Göttingen, 1931.
5. *The Knowledge of God and the Service of God According to the Teaching of the Reformation* (Gifford Lectures), New York, 1939, p. 20.
6. Ibid. p. 26.
7. Ibid. p. 9.
8. *The Idea of the Holy. An Inquiry into the non-Rational Factor in the Idea of the Divine and its Relation to the Rational,* tr. J. W. Harvey, London, 1936.
9. *Agape and Eros. A Study of the Christian Idea of Love,* tr. by A. G. Hebert, London, 1941, 3 vols.
10. *Christianity and Classical Culture,* Oxford, 1940.
11. *God in Christian Experience,* New York, London, n.d., p. 110.
12. *Die Lehre von Gott (Die Kirchliche Dogmatik,* II, 1), Zürich, 1946, pp. 210-13. The dependence of Barth's position upon modern criticism, which is suggested by the following argument, has been established from a very different point of view by Cornelius Van Til in *The New Modern-*

ism. An Appraisal of the Theology of Barth and Brunner, 2nd ed., Philadelphia, 1947.

13. *Die Lehre von Gott (Dogmatik*, II, 1), p. 92.

14. Ibid. p. 90.

15. Horace, *Epistles*, I, 10, 24.

16. *The Doctrine of the Trinity*, New York, 1944.

17. *The Doctrine of the Word of God*, p. 383.

18. *Die Lehre von Gott*, II, 1, p. 88.

19. Ibid. p. 89.

20. Ibid. p. 8.

21. *Metaphysics*, 1074 b 34 (XII, ch. 9).

22. 'Protestantism in the Present World-Situation,' *American Journal of Sociology* XLIII (1937/8), pp. 236-48.

23. *Die Lehre von Gott (Die Kirchliche Dogmatik*, II, 2), p. 822.

24. It is characteristic that one of Heidegger's disciples has given us a penetrating and sympathetic analysis of the Gnostic world-picture; *cf.* H. Jonas, *Gnosis und spätantiker Geist*, Göttingen, 1934.

25. *Enneades*, II, 9.

26. *De civitate Dei*, VII, 29.

27. *Die Lehre von Gott (Die Kirchliche Dogmatik*, II, 2), pp. 34-5.

28. Pascal founded a transport society, patented by the King and licensed by Parliament on 7 February, 1662. French bus services were actually organized at this time in accordance with Pascal's ideas. Cf. Jaques Chevalier, *Pascal*, Paris, 1922, p. 160.

29. *Die Lehre von Gott (Die Kirchliche Dogmatik*, II, 2) p. 35.

30. *Agape and Eros*, vol. I, p. 171. The two recent works on Christian love which seem of greatest importance to the writer include a criticism of Nygren that is generally in accord with the view expressed here. I refer to John Burnaby, *Amor Dei, a Study of the Religion of St. Augustine*, London, 1938, and M. C. D'Arcy, *The Mind and Heart of Love. A Study in Eros and Agape*, New York, 1947.

31. 29 e.

32. Mt. v.48.

33. I Cor. IX.24.

34. Op. cit. p. 54.

35. 803 c; cf. 644 d and 804 c.

36. *Adv. haer.*, IV, 20, 7.